WRITERS AND THEIR WORK

ISOBEL ARMSTRONG
General Editor

THE IMAGIST POETS

THE IMAGIST POETS

Andrew Thacker

© Copyright 2011 Andrew Thacker

First published in 2011 by Northcote House Publishers Ltd, Horndon, Tavistock, Devon, PL19 9NQ, United Kingdom.
Tel: +44 (0) 1822 810066 Fax: +44 (0) 1822 810034.

All rights reserved. No part of this work may be reproduced or stored in an information retrieval system (other than short extracts for the purposes of review) without the express permission of the Publishers given in writing.

British Library Cataloguing-in-Publication Data
A catalogue record for this book is available from the British Library

ISBN 978-0-7463-1062-5 hardcover
ISBN 978-0-7463-1002-1 paperback

Typeset by PDQ Typesetting, Newcastle-under-Lyme
Printed and bound in the United Kingdom

For Moya

Contents

Acknowledgements	viii
Biographical Outlines	ix
Abbreviations	xiii
Introduction: The Formation of Imagism	1
1 Movements and Modernism	10
2 Publishing, Publicity, and Magazines	24
3 Prefaces and Manifestos	37
4 Modern Themes	53
5 Urban Images	67
6 Gender and Sexuality: 'Amygism' and 'H.D. Imagiste'	89
Afterword	102
Notes	109
Select Bibliography	124
Index	131

Acknowledgements

I would like to thank Isobel Armstrong and Brian Hulme for commissioning this book, and for their patience in waiting for its completion. Over a number of years I have benefited enormously from conversations and advice upon Imagism from Helen Carr, and in particular from reading in manuscript her brilliant group biography of the Imagists, *The Verse Revolutionaries*. Many other friends and colleagues have provided helpful advice or comments, including Rebecca Beasley, Melissa Bradshaw, Peter Brooker, Andrzej Gasiorek, and Scott McCracken. My colleagues at De Montfort University, Leicester, have also provided a supportive environment in which to complete the book. And love and thanks, as always, to Moya and Daniel for their very particular forms of advice and criticism.

Biographical Outlines

1874   Amy Lowell born 9 February at Brookline, Massachusetts, youngest child of Augustus Lowell and Katherine Bigelow Lawrence Lowell.
1883   Thomas Ernest Hulme born 16 September at Gratton Hall, Endon, Staffordshire, eldest child of Thomas Hulme, a gentleman farmer, and Mary Young.
1885   Ezra Loomis Pound born 30 October at Hailey, Idaho, USA, the only child of Homer Loomis Pound, assayer, and his wife, Isabella. Frank Stewart Flint born 19 December at 117 Barnsbury Road in Islington, London, one of several children of William Thomas Flint, a commercial traveller, and his wife, Hannah Alice Tricker.
1886   John Gould Fletcher born 3 January in Little Rock, Arkansas, USA, second child of John Gould and Adolphine Krause Fletcher. H.D. (Hilda Doolittle) born 10 September at 11 Church Street, Bethlehem, Pennsylvania, USA, the second of the four children of the astronomer Charles Leander Doolittle and his second wife, Helen Wolle.
1892   Richard Aldington (christened Edward Godfree) born 8 July at 50 High Street, Portsmouth, the eldest among the two sons and two daughters of Albert Edward Aldington, bookseller and stationer, and later solicitor's clerk and amateur author, and Jessie May Godfree.
1901   H.D. meets Pound in Philadelphia, while he is a student at the University of Pennsylvania.
1905   H.D. and Pound become engaged; broken off in the next three years.
1908   Pound leaves America for Europe, settling in London. Publishes *A Lume Spento* in Venice. Fletcher sails from America for Trieste in August, then Rome in November,

	before settling in London in May 1909. Flint begins to write for Orage's magazine *The New Age*. Hulme joins the Poets' Club, a members' group in central London; delivers 'A Lecture on Modern Poetry' to the club.
1909	Pound publishes *Personae*. Flint publishes *In the Net of the Stars*. Hulme publishes 'Autumn' and 'A City Sunset' in a booklet of the Poets' Club, *For Christmas*. This is critically reviewed by Flint and leads to a new group of poets, led by Hulme, meeting at the Tour Eiffel restaurant in March. Begins articles on Bergson for *The New Age*. Pound meets W. B. Yeats, Ford Madox Ford, and T. E. Hulme (the latter at a Tour Eiffel meeting in April).
1910	Pound first contributes to *The New Age*.
1911	H.D. travels to Europe with her mother and friend Frances Gregg. H.D. stays in London when the others return to the America.
1912	H.D. meets Aldington and they are married the following year. Pound publishes *Ripostes* and is appointed 'foreign correspondent' of *Poetry* (Chicago) magazine; Pound writes 'H.D. Imagiste' on poems by H.D., probably in British Museum teashop. Lowell publishes *A Dome of Many-Coloured Glass*. Meets actress Ada Dwyer Russell in March who lives with Lowell from June 1914. Flint publishes his important article 'Contemporary French Poetry' in *Poetry Review*. Hulme publishes his 'Complete Poetical Works' in *The New Age*. Fletcher settles in London after visiting Paris and Italy.
1913	Publication of first critical pieces on Imagist ideas: 'Imagisme' and 'A Few Don'ts by an Imagiste'. H.D. publishes first poems in *Poetry*, January. Lowell travels to London and meets Aldington, H.D., Fletcher, and Pound. Pound meets Mary Fenollosa and is invited to edit her late husband's papers. Fletcher finances the publication of five volumes of his poetry: *The Dominant City; Fool's Gold; Fire and Wine; The Book of Nature; Visions of the Evening*. Pound persuades him to provide money for contributors to *The New Freewoman/Egoist* magazine.
1914	*Des Imagistes* published, edited by Pound. Two infamous dinners to celebrate Vorticism and Imagism held in July at Dieudonné's restaurant, London. At the second, Pound parodies Lowell's verse, marking the split within

Imagism between these two. Pound marries Dorothy Shakespear in April. Meets T. S. Eliot in September. Shifts allegiance from Imagism to the Vorticism of Wyndham Lewis. Lowell publishes *Sword Blades and Poppy Seed*; arranges for the publication of future Imagist anthologies, but without Pound. Hulme enlists in the army at the outbreak of war in August. Fletcher returns to America at outbreak of war; studies Oriental art in Boston.

1915 *Some Imagist Poets 1915* published. Aldington publishes *Images, 1910–15* and becomes literary editor of *The Egoist*. Pound publishes *Cathay*. Flint publishes *Cadences*. Fletcher publishes *Irradiations: Sand and Spray*.

1916 *Some Imagist Poets 1916* published. Aldington joins the army in June and serves at the front until the war is over, suffering from traumatic stress in later years. H.D. publishes *Sea Garden*, her first volume of poems; substitutes for Aldington for a year as assistant editor at *The Egoist*. Lowell publishes *Men, Women and Ghosts*. Travels across America over next two years giving lectures on the 'New Poetry'. Pound publishes *Lustra*. Fletcher returns to England; publishes *Goblins and Pagodas*.

1917 *Some Imagist Poets 1917* published. Lowell publishes *Tendencies in Modern American Poetry*. Pound publishes first versions of the *Cantos* in *Poetry*. Hulme dies, killed in action near Nieuport in Flanders on 26 September. H.D. publishes *The Tribute and Circe: Two Poems*.

1918 H.D. becomes pregnant with the child of composer Cecil Gray, born as Frances Perdita Aldington in 1919; separates from Aldington but is not divorced until 1938; meets Bryher (Winifred Ellerman) her lifelong companion. Bryher publishes *Amy Lowell: A Critical Appreciation*. Lowell publishes *Can Grande's Castle*. Flint conscripted into army. Fletcher publishes *Japanese Prints*.

1919 Aldington publishes *Images of War*. Lowell publishes *Pictures of the Floating World*.

1920 Pound leaves London for Paris; publishes the poem *Hugh Selwyn Mauberley* as a 'farewell' to London. Flint publishes *Otherworld: Cadences*, his last work of poetry. Works in the British Civil Service until retirement in

	1951, publishes articles and translations for various journals. Fletcher returns to America.
1921	Lowell publishes *Legends* and *Fir-Flower Tablets* (with Florence Ayscough). H.D. publishes *Hymen*.
1923	H.D. publishes *Heliodora and Other Poems*. Pound settles in Rapallo, Italy. Hulme's posthumous essays, *Speculations*, published.
1924	Lowell dies of a stroke, while at home in Brookline. Her *What's O' Clock* is posthumously awarded Pulitzer Prize.
1925	H.D. publishes *Collected Poems*.
1926	H.D. composes *Bid Me to Live* (unpublished until 1960), a fictional account of Aldington, D. H. Lawrence and herself in wartime London.
1928	Aldington publishes anti-war novel, *Death of A Hero*.
1929	*Imagist Anthology 1930* published, with foreword by Ford Madox Ford.
1930	Glenn Hughes publishes *Imagism and the Imagists: A Study in Modern Poetry*, the first critical work on the movement.
1932	H.D. in analysis with Freud in Vienna, an event later portrayed in her *Tribute to Freud* (1956).
1937	Fletcher publishes autobiography, *Life Is My Song*.
1941	Aldington publishes autobiography, *Life for Life's Sake*.
1950	Fletcher dies, committing suicide in Arkansas.
1960	Flint dies in Harwell, Berkshire.
1961	H.D. dies in Zurich.
1962	Aldington dies in the south of France.
1972	Pound dies in Venice.

Abbreviations

CPW	Amy Lowell, *The Complete Poetical Works of Amy Lowell* (Boston: Houghton Mifflin, 1955)
DI	*Des Imagistes: An Anthology* (London: Poetry Bookshop, 1914)
FS	T. E. Hulme, *Further Speculations*, ed. Samuel Hynes (Minneapolis: University of Minnesota Press, 1955)
IP	*Imagist Poetry*, ed. Peter Jones (Harmondsworth: Penguin, 1972)
S	T. E. Hulme, *Speculations: Essays on Humanism and the Philosophy of Art*, ed. Herbert Read (London: Routledge and Kegan Paul, 1924)
SIP 1915	*Some Imagist Poets 1915: An Anthology* (Boston and New York: Houghton Mifflin, 1915)
SIP 1916	*Some Imagist Poets 1916: An Annual Anthology* (Boston and New York: Houghton Mifflin, 1916)
SIP 1917	*Some Imagist Poets 1917: An Annual Anthology* (Boston and New York: Houghton Mifflin, 1917)
SW	T. E. Hulme, *Selected Writings*, ed. Patrick McGuinness (Manchester: Carcanet, 1998)

Introduction: The Formation of Imagism

Imagism has often been regarded by literary history as one of the founding moments of modern poetry, as a significant presence within Anglo-American modernism, and as an important influence upon the development of experimental and avant-garde poetry in English throughout the twentieth century. Looking back from the 1950s T. S. Eliot, for example, wrote that 'the starting point of modern poetry is the group denominated "imagists" in London about 1910'.[1] Eliot's judgement was upheld in one of the first and most influential accounts of modern poetry after the Second World War, C. K. Stead's *The New Poetic* (1964); their status was then confirmed in the enduring anthology of the poets, *Imagist Poetry*, edited by Peter Jones and published by Penguin in 1972. This collection is still in print over thirty years later and is probably the first encounter with Imagism for many readers.

But who were the Imagist poets and why is it still worth reading them today, in the twenty-first century? Should they not be considered merely a footnote in literary history, or perhaps a minor chapter in any study of literary modernism in the early years of the twentieth century? This book suggests that it is still of interest to read the Imagist poets, and to evaluate their role within a wider narrative of British and American modernism. Their impact, therefore, deserves something more than cursory notes or summary chapters.

The Imagists consisted of a central core of Richard Aldington, H.D. (Hilda Doolittle), John Gould Fletcher, F. S. Flint, Amy Lowell and Ezra Pound. Other writers published in the anthologies included D. H. Lawrence, James Joyce, William

Carlos Williams, and Ford Madox Ford. There were five anthologies of Imagist poetry, in 1914, 1915, 1916, 1917 and a retrospective one in 1930. Imagism helped launch the careers, in particular, of Pound, H.D. and Amy Lowell, and provided a set of statements for the reform of poetic language that influenced many other modernist writers, and later poets.

Conventionally Ezra Pound has been viewed as the central figure behind the theory and practice of Imagist poetry. Pound, critics have suggested, 'invented' Imagism in order to further his career, and that of others, in a cultural environment where many other artistic 'isms' such as Cubism, Futurism or Impressionism jostled for space and public attention. Pound, in this version of the story, then tired of Imagism and moved off to found another artistic movement, Vorticism, with the painter and writer Percy Wyndham Lewis. When Pound left the group after the first anthology in 1914 Imagism declined in power and stature, and became merely a watered down version of the avant-garde literary movement Pound conceived in 1910.

This book will offer a different narrative to the one sketched above. It will show the variety of practice within the Imagist group, and shift the focus from seeing Imagism purely as the creation of Pound. This will be done by granting a much stronger focus to often overlooked figures such as Lowell, Flint, and Fletcher. Lowell's role in the maintenance and promotion of Imagism has been ignored by a literary history that follows the story told by Pound of a 'dilution' of the 'hard light, clear edges' of Imagism. Likewise, the experimental poetry of the city by Fletcher, and the 'polyphonic prose' of Lowell deserve far greater attention than they have so far received. Since the publication of her *Collected Poems* in 1983 H.D.'s contribution to Imagism has also received more attention, particularly within feminist work on modernism.

To concentrate upon individual figures and their merits is always necessary when considering stylistic innovations within the history of poetry. Reconsidering the value of a poet like Lowell is also a worthwhile strategy given ongoing debates around the literary canon within English studies. But such a revisioning of the place of Imagist writers within modernism fails to address one of the most fascinating and, until relatively recently, most overlooked features of modernism: the *group* identity of Imagism. In the construction of a group of writers with a supposedly shared agenda that could be labelled 'Imagism', the Imagist poets provided one model of how an artistic movement might present itself in the crowded marketplace of early modernism. One of the innovations of this book will be a focus upon the *cultural formation* of Imagism as a movement competing within the artistic avant-garde of Britain and America.[2] Lawrence Rainey's provocative account in the *Institutions of Modernism* (1998) has drawn attention to the question of *where* and *how* modernist movements such as Imagism emerged in the aggressive and highly competitive social and cultural environment of the early twentieth century. For Rainey, Imagism represents an 'anti-avant-garde' movement when compared to the Italian artistic movement of Futurism, which, led by F. T. Marinetti, created a whirl of publicity across Europe before 1914. Such a judgement raises the question of how we describe the nature of the Imagist group as a literary movement, as avant-garde or not, and what we might mean by an avant-garde poetry in English. Later chapters in this book will not only focus on the poetic texts of Imagist, but will also scrutinize such features as the format of the Prefaces or manifestos of Imagist theory, and the role of little magazines (such as *The Egoist* and *Poetry*) and the publishing industry in promoting Imagism. By drawing attention to such *institutions* of literature, as Rainey terms them, we will gain a greater sense of the Imagist poets as a group rather than merely as a slightly quarrelsome bunch of individuals.

It is useful, then, to outline the publication history of Imagism in order to start to consider the collective identity of Imagism, before examining stylistically what an early twentieth-century reader could expect from an Imagist poem in 1914, and how it might differ from other poetry of the period. Of the five anthologies, only the first contained work by Ezra Pound, a fact that has perhaps not been stressed enough in histories of Imagism that give the lead to Pound. This anthology was called, *Des Imagistes, An Anthology*, and was also edited by Pound. It first appeared in the February 1914 edition of the American little magazine *The Glebe* and was subsequently issued as a book in March of that year in America, and in London in April under the auspices of the Poetry Bookshop. The transnational nature of the publication of Imagism, sometimes overlooked, is another significant feature of the group that informs the character of its modernism.

The poets included in Des Imagistes were Richard Aldington, H.D., F. S. Flint, Skipworth Cannell, Amy Lowell, William Carlos Williams, James Joyce, Pound, Ford Madox Ford, Allen Upward, and John Cournos. Of these writers only four were allowed more than a single poem (Aldington, Flint, H.D., and Pound), indicating those whom Pound considered the core members of the group. Indeed, it is hard to justify – even with the most permissive of definitions – the description of Imagist for certain of the poems, such as Joyce's rather leaden 'I Hear an Army': 'I hear an army charging upon the land,/ And the thunder of horses plunging; foam about their knees'. With its traditional use of metre, stanza, and rhyme, this poem demonstrates that the term 'Imagism' signified more than simply an experimental form of verse; 'Imagism' signified a new modern movement as much as a new poetic style, and, arguably, it was the movement which defined the style rather than vice-versa. The inclusion in the anthology of an unmodern, and probably non-Imagist, poem by a 'modern' writer, such as Joyce, indicates a complex set of issues around cultural value, the promotion of individual careers, the advertising function of anthologies, and the nature of this modernism at this point in time. As Rainey asks of Pound's machinations in the inauguration of Imagism, is it simply to be regarded as the 'launching and marketing of a new product'?[3] These issues will be considered further in chapters 1 and 2.

The next three Imagist volumes, respectively *Some Imagist Poets: An Anthology* of 1915, 1916, and 1917, were published under arrangements negotiated by Amy Lowell, the Boston-born poet who had met Pound in London in 1913. For these volumes two new 'Imagists' were added: the English D. H. Lawrence and the American John Gould Fletcher. Aldington, Lowell, Flint, and H.D. were retained, but all other contributors to *Des Imagistes* were dropped. This diminution to a group of only six writers who published collectively for three years produced an image of coherence and continuity for the movement, even if stylistically there were still major differences between members. To emphasize this manifestation of coherence, the later anthologies each included an anonymous Preface, probably written by Lowell, Aldington, and Fletcher, purporting to spell out the Imagist doctrine in further detail for the puzzled reader. Chapter 3 will analyse these documents and other contemporary critical essays by the poets for what they can tell us about Imagist theory.

Lowell's stewardship of these anthologies resulted in impressive sales and publicity for the new poetry of Imagism, especially in America where she gave numerous readings to promote the work. An indication of this is that the 1915 anthology went into three editions, and the 1916 into two.[4] In 1930 Aldington, together with Ford Madox Ford and H.D., produced the *Imagist Anthology 1930*. This contained all of the original contributors except, in Aldington's words, 'poor Amy who was dead, Skipwith [sic] Cannell who we couldn't trace, and Ezra who was sulky'.[5]

The grounds for Pound's sulky attitude to Imagist publications originated in his absence from the 1915 anthology. By September 1914 Lowell and Pound had quarrelled, ostensibly over Pound's autocratic editorial style. In reality, the quarrel was over the leadership and 'ownership' of the movement. Lowell, made suspicious of Pound by John Gould Fletcher, suggested to Pound that *Des Imagistes* was 'too monotonous and too undemocratic in that certain poets were allowed more space than others' and that in the future poets themselves should be allowed to choose their own contributions to the anthologies. Pound's response, wrote Lowell, was blackmail: 'he would only join us on condition that I would obligate myself to give $200 a year to some indigent poet...I absolutely refused to be intimidated into buying anything, or to buy his poems at the expense of my self-respect'.[6] Pound's view was that Lowell had hijacked his poetic movement and, more heinously, had distorted the meaning of the word 'Imagism'. Pound wrote tetchily to Lowell in August 1914:

> I should like the name 'Imagisme' to retain some sort of a meaning. It stands, or I should like it to stand for hard light, clear edges. I can not trust any democratized committee to maintain that standard. Some will be splay-footed and some sentimental.[7]

Lowell might well have retorted that Pound's control over standards was no guarantee of quality given some of the contributions to *Des Imagistes*. Joyce's 'I Hear an Army' might not have been 'splay-footed', whatever that might mean, but it could well be accused of being sentimental and lacking in 'hard light', especially with its closing lines: 'My heart, have you no wisdom thus to despair?/ My love, my love, my love, why have you left me alone?'

The Pound/Lowell dispute, therefore, can be understood as a clash of personalities and politics as much as a disagreement over poetic principles. Pound continued to complain of Lowell in his letters until early in 1915 when he wrote to Harriet Monroe, editor of the magazine *Poetry*, that he had finally broken with Lowell and her forthcoming *Some Imagist Poets 1915* because she sought 'to turn "Imagism" into a democratic beergarden'.[8] Such disputes and disagreements may often occur among writers, and indeed anyone, with strong personalities and ideas, but the clash between Pound and Lowell indicates something more than these commonplaces about human behaviour. For the argument takes us to the heart of questions central to Imagism or any group that functions as a cultural formation: how are individual identities to be negotiated within a group identity, and how is the collective nature of the group to be articulated, maintained, and presented to the wider world? For Pound the group was organized by a central leader, who maintained the 'clear edges' of what Imagism entailed, the phrase itself perhaps more applicable to the notion of a party membership than a poetic style. For Lowell the movement was still to be organized around a central figure, herself, but with a different model (more 'democratic') for the interaction of the group members. If the reading public were puzzled by what Imagism meant, Pound was none too bothered, believing the vocation of the modernist group to be primarily that of a literary vanguard for establishing the careers of writers. Lowell saw Imagism as something that needed to be explained to a bewildered public: her public readings, lectures, and writings testified to a different mission envisaged for Imagism. Overall, these different options for Imagism can be judged as diverse strategies for establishing and maintaining a cultural movement within modernism. Examining how these strategies operated, and what their implications were, will be a central aim of this book.

However, a focus upon the institutions of modernism such as publishing and little magazines must be related both to particular aesthetic styles of the Imagist poets and to their personalities and artistic temperaments. This is why I use the term cultural formation to describe Imagism, as a description of the specific forms and styles of Imagist poems, as well as a term capturing the processes that impelled the group into being, and which governed their relationships with one another within the group. To talk about the Imagists as a cultural formation is therefore to try to link together the social, cultural, and economic history of modernism during the period of the anthologies, the character of relationships within the group, and the artistic forms and practices that they espoused. Only in this way can we gain a fuller picture of the 'new product' that was Imagism.

To conclude this introduction I want to turn to the stylistic innovations of Imagist poetry, having spent some time sketching out the issues surrounding the group identity of them as a formation. A reader encountering Imagism for the first time in 1914 would have contrasted such poetry with what was more familiar amongst contemporary verse. Here is an extract from a poem, 'Sunset in the City', by Richard Le Gallienne, an English poet of the 1890s. Le Gallienne's poetry is associated with the literary style known as Symbolism, which, by 1914, was a fairly recognizable style of writing in English:

> Above the town a monstrous wheel is turning,
> With glowing spokes of red,
> Low in the west its fiery axle burning;
> And, lost amid the spaces overhead,
> A vague white moth, the moon, is fluttering.
>
> Above the town an azure sea is flowing,
> 'Mid long peninsulas of shining sand,
> From opal unto pearl the moon is growing,
> Dropped like a shell upon the changing strand.[9]

'Sunset in the City' is, to an extent, a successful evocation of its subject matter, one of a number of poems by Le Gallienne and other poets around the turn of the century that depict urban themes, especially based on London. However, the formal techniques used here are very conventional ones that can be found in much English poetry over the previous hundred years or more: the poem has a tight metrical pattern (roughly iambic pentameters), a familiar rhyme scheme, and a use of syntactic devices that are also conventional ('fiery axle burning' is often described as a Miltonic construction). None of these features make this a bad poem, but to the Imagist poet desperate to be seen as avant-garde this would be an example of 'dated' poetry. Consider Richard Aldington's poem 'Sunsets', from the 1916 *Some Imagist Poets*, which takes a similar subject matter to that of Le Gallienne:

> The white body of the evening
> Is torn into scarlet,
> Slashed and gouged and seared
> Into crimson,
> And hung ironically
> With garlands of mist.
> And the wind
> Blowing over London from Flanders
> Has a bitter taste.

(*SIP 1916* 10)

Formally this poem departs markedly from the earlier text. There is no regular rhyme, metre or stanza – it is clearly an example of *vers libre*, or free verse, one of the most distinctive characteristics of much modernist poetry. The syntax has no inversions such as 'fiery axle burning' and mostly follows the quality of speech, especially the use of 'And' to start a sentence. Comparing the central trope of the sky in both poems is also instructive: Le Gallienne's moon is compared to a 'vague white moth' amidst a sky marked by the red tones of the setting sun, described in turn by a series of terms: 'monstrous', 'glowing', and the burning axle. Tellingly, Le Gallienne feels the need to spell out to the reader that the fluttering white moth is actually the moon. Aldington's imagery is sharper, short, and generally more allusive; the evening sky is compared to a body violently attacked, but the simile is a suppressed one – Aldington does not write, for example, that the evening sky *is like* a human body. The visual imagery here seems more controlled and integrated into the subject matter of the poem than in Le Gallienne. The red and white colouring implies a bloodied body, revealed at the end of the poem to be connected with the 'bitter' wind from the First World War battlefields of Flanders. In contrast one is unsure why Le Gallienne's sunset evinces such fiery and monstrous characteristics.

Aldington served in the infantry during the war, and returned suffering from shell-shock. Imagism is not often considered in terms of being 'First World War poetry' (although a fair number of anthologized poems did address the war), but here the sombre subject matter is reflected in the more brutal language of the text. In Imagist terms Aldington's poem is the more 'direct' of the two, it presents its imagery in what Pound referred to as a 'direct treatment of the thing'. One could query whether the repetition of terms to imply attack – torn, slashed, gouged, and seared – is strictly necessary, given the Imagist dictum 'To use absolutely no word that did not contribute to the presentation'. Aldington's defence might have been that the intensity and prolonged quality of violence after three years of war needed to be presented and therefore could only be captured in these repeated synonyms.

It is useful, then, to notice the differences between these two poems without discussing at this point the complexities and contradictions of Imagist theory. Roughly two decades apart, these two poems demonstrate a vastly altered strategy around verse-form and technique. There are many explanations for this transformation in English verse in this period – from the impact of French poets in the English-speaking world, to the changing social and political landscape facing the modern poet – but in the next chapter I want to focus further upon how the stylistic innovations of Imagism were intertwined with its self-definition as a modernist movement.[10]

1

Movements and Modernism

The founding of the Imagist movement has been discussed many times and, not surprisingly, has engendered different recollections by the central protagonists. The primal scene of the founding seems to have been the 1912 meeting in a teashop in Kensington, London (or possibly a café in or near the British Museum), between Pound, Aldington and H.D. Pound praised a sheaf of new poems by H.D. and wrote, 'H.D. Imagiste' at the bottom of the manuscript.[1] Aldington and H.D., by all accounts, seemed rather puzzled by this term, but were willing to collude with the new movement, particularly as Pound could get their work published in the new American magazine *Poetry* and, noted Aldington, 'nobody else at that time would look at them'.[2] According to F. S. Flint, Pound derived the name by combining T. E. Hulme's idea of the 'image' (itself originating in the philosopher Bergson) and an article by Flint in *The Poetry Review* where he discussed various groups in contemporary French poetry.[3] Aside from French models of literary 'movements', the idea of a group of poets publishing in a collective manifestation had several precursors in London at this time. One example known to Pound through his friendship with Yeats would have been the Rhymers' Club who met to read and discuss poetry at Ye Olde Cheshire Cheese pub in Fleet Street, London, in the 1890s and who published two anthologies of poetry as *The Book of the Rhymers' Club*. A more immediate link to the Imagists was the Poets' Club, which met in a relatively formal setting in London's Mayfair, with Hulme as its honorary secretary, and whose 1908 volume of poems was reviewed by Flint. Hulme and Flint then led a breakaway faction from this earlier group and decided to meet more informally. This group met on Thursday evenings from March 1909 onwards at the Tour Eiffel restaurant, off Tottenham Court Road and its members included Hulme, Desmond Fitzgerald, Flint, Edward Storer, Florence Farr, Francis Tancred, and Joseph Campbell. Pound first attended on 22 April 1909. The members read and corrected each other's verse, discussed *vers libre* and the idea of adapting Japanese and Hebrew forms for the composition of English poetry. Pound wrote that the Imagists were descended from this 'forgotten school of 1909', a group he described as the 'School of Images'.[4]

The fact that in 1912 Aldington and H.D. agreed to be termed Imagists, along with the other contributors to *Des Imagistes* gathered together by Pound, can best be understood in terms of the cultural politics of the various literary movements in this period, rather than simply as the force of a single personality or adherence to a particular style or ism. Becoming an Imagist poet did not necessarily entail a detailed understanding of Imagist theory; sometimes it implied merely that one welcomed publishing under a collective banner. Flint, for example, in a retrospective judgement after Imagism's demise, claimed that 'We had a doctrine of the image, which none of us knew anything about'.[5] Disingenuous as this might be, given Flint's knowledge of how T. E. Hulme had theorized the role of the image in poetry, it does indicates something significant about the character of the Imagists as a modernist grouping. Part of the function of movements, as Aldington's comment above emphasizes, was the fact that they seemed crucial in getting one's work published. We can learn much about how movements such as Imagism functioned by considering the overlaps between it and other cultural formations such as the Georgian poets or the Italian Futurists.

Douglas Goldring, in a literary memoir of this period, noted that what he recalled most about 'the crowded years between 1910 and 1914' were 'the exciting series of art movements' in which writers and artists in London got caught up.[6] In these years an aspiring artist or writer in London could consider forming an allegiance to any one, or more, of a dazzling array of isms: Post-Impressionism (first unleashed upon the British public with the famous exhibition of 1910); Futurism (launched in 1909 in Paris by the Italian Filippo Marinetti, who controversially lectured upon it in London in 1910, 1912, and 1914); Impressionism (which began in the nineteenth century with French painters but was adopted as a literary term by novelists such as Joseph Conrad and Ford Madox Ford); Symbolism (a movement that traversed painting, music, and literature, discussed by Arthur Symons in his book of 1899 but possibly passé by 1910); Vorticism (founded by Wyndham Lewis, with Pound, as an English avant-garde counterblast to Italian Futurism); Unanimisme (if one was aware of French poets such as Jules Romains, as Flint was, writing an article on this ism in 1912); or Cubism (but perhaps only by acquaintance with painting in Paris at the time or by a reader of a modernist magazine like *The New Age* which reviewed such trends). Expressionism, Surrealism, Objectivism, Constructivism, and many others, were soon to follow in the wake of these modernist formations.[7] It is not surprising that Ford Madox Ford, writing a foreword to the *Imagist Anthology* of 1930, recollected that 'It is a little difficult to disentangle Futurism from Cubism and Vorticism and Imagism and indeed, even from Impressionism and Post Impressionism and Dadaism and Hyper-realism. At least it isn't now. But in those days it was bewildering'.[8] Even today, contemporary students using the enduring Penguin anthology of *Imagist Poetry* by Peter Jones are often equally disorientated by the fact that the book's cover has in different editions featured paintings by William Roberts and Wyndham Lewis – aren't they Vorticists and not Imagists note some attentive readers?[9]

Bewildering it might have been, but belonging to some such association was almost essential for artists and writers at the time. The apparent necessity for an individual to join with other like-minded modernists is indicated simply by some of the oddities of group membership. As noted in the introduction, a poem by Joyce was included in the first Imagist anthology, although the epithet 'Imagism' fits neither the poem nor the author. It is arguable whether D. H. Lawrence's poetry, which appeared in the next three compilations but not in the first, can count as Imagist, considered stylistically – and Lawrence never saw himself as an Imagist member. The terse poetry of T. E. Hulme, often considered exemplary for its Imagist concision, appeared in none of the anthologies. In order to make sense of such peculiarities it is necessary to understand why a writer felt impelled to join an ism or to be published in the anthology of an ism.

From around the end of the nineteenth century the social and economic conditions that dominated artistic production resulted in writers and artists feeling the need to band together in various isms and movements. Changes in the structure of Victorian culture from the middle of the nineteenth century resulted in artists and writers being distanced from their position at the centre of society. This shift might be understood as one where the idea of the poet Tennyson as a sage, able to speak and be heard by a broad public on matters of national interest, was replaced by the poet as part of an embattled minority, separated from the majority of the reading public. The desire to shock the public, to *épater les bourgeois*, as became fashionable in the 1880s and 1890s with Oscar Wilde's decadence and Walter Pater's aestheticism, was part of this separation between mainstream culture and the artistic minority.[10] While serious writing went in one direction, into what seemed to some to be a coterie of misunderstood poets writing deliberately obtuse poems, other writers moved towards the new cultural market opened by cheaper printing costs, the growth of mass circulation newspapers, and the idea of the writer as a paid professional.

George Gissing's novel, *New Grub Street* (1891), is the classic statement of this new aesthetic dichotomy at the turn of the nineteenth century. The novel dramatizes the division between literary value and the market value of literature in the tale of two writers, Jasper Milvain and Edwin Reardon. Reardon struggles to maintain literary standards by composing traditional novels rather than writing shorter paid pieces for the new periodical press; he refuses to 'make a trade of an art'.[11] In contrast Milvain declares, 'I shall never write for writing's sake, only to make money. All my plans and efforts will have money in view'.[12] Early on in the novel Jasper sums up the difference between the two writers:

> He [Reardon] is the old type of unpractical artist; I am the literary man of 1882. He won't make concessions, or rather, he can't make them; he can't supply the market.... Literature nowadays is a trade. Putting aside men of genius, who may succeed by mere cosmic force, your successful man of letters is your skilful tradesman. He thinks first and foremost of the markets; when one kind of goods begins to go off slackly, he is ready with something new and appetising.[13]

Faced with this ruthlessly economic vision of writing, an alternative strategy began to appear to certain artists. If one could afford to, one might reject the mainstream literary market altogether and form common allegiance with other like-minded individuals. One now did not supply artistic products for a mainstream market, one wrote instead either for oneself or for a small group, a clique or coterie of sympathetic readers, who were often fellow writers. Thus, as part of a beleaguered and resentful minority, writers and artists grouped together for support and solidarity: that the public did not understand the 'new art' of Post-Impressionism, or found Imagist verse puzzling in its lack of metre and rhyme, only confirmed this divergence between a mass culture and that of a minority. The significant modernist little magazine, *The Little Review*, summed up this parting of the ways with its masthead slogan: 'Making No Compromise with the Public Taste'.

Yet this account of the emergence of a split between high and low culture, or between mass and minority culture, has been challenged by much recent scholarship on modernism. Critics such as Michael North, Mark Morrisson, and Lawrence Rainey have argued that modernism was not endemically opposed to the new mass culture; rather, modernism was deeply entangled with the practices of the mass market for culture.[14] One example with a clear relevance for Imagism, discussed in the next chapter, is the use of little magazines for publication, themselves enabled by the same economic and technological conditions that allowed a paper like the *Daily Mail* to sell a million copies. Another point of comparison between the minority modernist and mass culture was the mutual employment of strategies such as marketing, advertising and publicity to 'sell' one's product. As Mark Morrisson argues, many artistic groups adapted 'commercial culture to the needs of modernist literature' and 'found the energies of promotional culture too attractive to ignore, especially when it came to advertising and publication techniques'. According to this argument, modernists did not simply embrace the mass market, but instead sought ways to adapt the 'promotional culture' of mass-market technologies and institutions to 'rejuvenate contemporary culture'.[15] They did not so much supply a pre-existing market, as Jasper Milvain in *New Grub Street* does, but tried to either influence the existing market or open up new alternative markets for experimental work. We can now understand the paradox of why individual writers joined forces with other writers to promote their careers via an aesthetic ism or cultural formation. Banding together via shared manifesto, group exhibition, and anthology or magazine publication bolstered promotion of one's own career. These are all examples of what Morrisson terms the 'promotional culture' of modernism – the product being both the shared ism and the individual artist. By 1914 this was a crowded marketplace with, as noted above, a mystifying range of isms from which the reading public could choose. There was, therefore, much jostling for position in this market, shown, for example, in the way that the Vorticist movement in its magazine, *Blast*, repeatedly tried to position itself as distinct from the seemingly competing movement of Futurism.[16] When considering linguistic style Pound counselled the Imagist poet to write in a clear, objective fashion: 'Consider the way of the scientist rather than the way of an advertising agent for a new soap'.[17] It would be more accurate to say that, although stylistically many Imagist poems followed this advice, the Imagist movement overall was precisely marketed as a new – but very poetic – type of soap.

The history of Imagism reveals both Ezra Pound and Amy Lowell as skilful promoters of the movement, as versions in fact of advertising agents. In his first contact with James Joyce, for example, Pound indicates that he can try to get the Irish writer published in various magazines with which he is connected. Some American magazines pay well, others less so, but, notes Pound, 'Appearance in the Egoist may have a slight advertisement value if you want to keep your name familiar'.[18] Soon after, early in 1914, Pound received Joyce's poem 'I Hear an Army' and agreed to publish it in *Des Imagistes*. Though Joyce was paid for the poem, the 'advertisement value' of the publication was clearly of more cultural value for an aspiring writer, as Pound was aware. Some years earlier Pound had written to his parents to encourage them to promote his early volume of poetry, *A Lume Spento*, back home in his native America: 'It pays to advertise, ergo spread this precious seed... What I want now is advance orders culled from general curiosity. The sale on pure & exalted merit will begin later Boom – Boom – cast delicacy to the wind for I must eat'.[19] Of course all writers like their work to be read, and most like to eat, but Pound's sense of the value of 'booming' literature was adapted to the Imagist movement as well. Calling this diverse bunch of poets Imagists marked them as a distinct product, the initial use of the French 'imagiste' form being the equivalent of gilding your new soap with an 'exotic' foreign name to catch the eye of the public. Pound was aware of the need for a name from the success of the 1912 Georgian anthology of poetry, published by Harold Monro, founder of an important meeting place for writers, the Poetry Bookshop. The first of five such anthologies, *Georgian Poetry* had by the end of 1913 sold around 9,000 copies, a fact Pound must have been aware of through his friendship with Monro and the fact that the editor of the anthology, Edward Marsh, had once considered publishing Pound in the collection.[20] Monro, after some reticence, did publish *Des Imagistes* in 1914, but unlike the Georgian volume, this sold badly. Perhaps the public did not take to the cryptic 'foreign' name, whereas the Georgian anthology could be taken to refer simply to the reign of the new monarch from 1910, George V. For a contemporary reader Georgian poems were also less puzzling than the short, epigrammatic styles typifying Imagist poetry, and with no explanatory preface in *Des Imagistes* (again unlike a short prefatory note by Marsh in the Georgian collection) the 'advertisement value' of appearing in the volume might be considered negligible.

Overlaps between the two formations can also be seen in Richard Aldington, who moved in Georgian circles, writing unpaid reviews for Harold Monro's magazine, *The Poetry Review*, a journal closely linked to the Georgian poets. In his autobiography Aldington refers to how he shifted allegiance from this group to another: 'At a "Dutch" Soho dinner [of Georgian poets] collected by Harold Monro, everyone was deploring Ezra and running him down'. Aldington finally rebelled and said Pound had more 'vitality in his little finger than the whole lot of you put together'. This, wrote Aldington, 'queered my pitch with a large and powerful clique, but I have never regretted it'. Clearly Aldington's lack of regret can be linked to his absorption into another modernist clique – the Imagists. Aldington's summary of the differences between the two poetic movements is interesting as an assessment of the character of the respective formations: 'The Georgians were regional in their outlook and in love with littleness'.[21] Pound, and the Imagists, notes Aldington, were more international in outlook, with Pound introducing Aldington to much European literature (much of which Pound himself had learnt from Flint). The Georgians, we might say, espoused a poetry of place, of a sense of belonging to a specific location, mainly that of a rural England (Housman and Shropshire; Edward Thomas and 'Adlestrop'; Brooke's corner of England). The Imagists were more poets of urban life, of London or Boston if any geography is mentioned, but also poets that drew upon non-English and non-European models – Chinese and Japanese styles in the case of Pound, Lowell and Fletcher, or the Ancient Greeks and Romans in the instance of H.D. and Aldington. Stylistically, then, the Georgians and Imagists differed; in terms of literary institutions there was overlap, demonstrated in the fact that Lawrence was published in both Georgian and Imagist anthologies, and that Monro was responsible for publishing the British version of *Des Imagistes*. Edward Marsh certainly perceived the Imagists to be a breakaway group from the Georgians. He wrote to the poet Rupert Brooke in June 1913: 'there's a movement for a "Post-Georgian" Anthology, of the Pound–Flint–Hulme school, who don't like being out of *GP* [Georgian Poetry] but I don't think it will come off'.[22]

If Aldington switched allegiance from the Georgians to the Imagists his attitude towards Futurism displays a more antagonistic stance. Marinetti, the founder of Futurism, had proposed a grey, utilitarian uniform for Futurist artists and Aldington wrote to Monro in May 1914: 'Are you going to Marinetti's lecture? I am preparing a costoom of violent green orange and blue for the occasion'.[23] Arguably, such hostility represents a grudging acknowledgement of the success of Futurism as an exemplary avant-garde movement in this period. Other Imagists were more welcoming to Marinetti at first. Flint had corresponded and met with Marinetti in 1912, taking him to visit Yeats when Marinetti visited London.[24] In 1913 Harold Monro had devoted an issue of his magazine *Poetry and Drama* to Futurism, being impressed that the Futurist poetry anthology had sold some 35,000 copies in Europe; later that year Marinetti spoke at the Poetry Bookshop.[25] Lawrence Rainey has argued that the sensational impact of Futurism caused Pound 'to launch Imagism in a more systematic and serious way'.[26] In particular Marinetti was an expert at promotional activities, utilizing interviews in the popular press and well-publicized appearances at key venues in London. Marinetti's success, suggests Rainey, forced 'intellectuals and artists to come to terms with the role of new institutions of mass culture and assess their bearings on the place of art in a cultural marketplace being radically transformed'.[27] For poets trying to establish themselves it now seemed even more important to present oneself as part of a group. However, Rainey argues that Pound's presentation of Imagism was much more tentative than that of Futurism, shown in his use of the term 'school' rather than 'movement', as deployed by Marinetti: 'Imagism rejected Futurism's ethos of collective identity: a school was something more informal, more casual, more individualistic'.[28] Although Pound claimed that Imagism was not 'a revolutionary school' and had published no 'manifesto', the difference Rainey draws between an Imagist school and a Futurist movement is perhaps too sharply delimited.[29] For example, Aldington noted that Pound often used the group as a way to exclude other figures: 'how often would Ezra obliterate a literary figure by the simple assertion: "*Il n'est pas dong le mouvemong*"'.[30] It was perhaps Lowell, rather than Pound, who more consistently used the term 'school', as in her reference in 1917 to 'the Imagist School' as a particular group within 'a larger, more comprehensive movement, the New Movement' that is yet to be named.[31] Certainly no explicitly Imagist 'manifesto' was published, but the function of articles by Pound, Flint, and later Lowell was precisely similar to that of such a manifesto, as is discussed in chapter 3.

To use Raymond Williams's vocabulary for describing modernism we can argue that both Imagism and Futurism were *cultural formations* within modernism, sharing many things and differing in others. Williams's schema for cultural formations is very helpful for distinguishing between the panoply of modernist isms. Williams characterizes such formations in two main ways: first, by noting different types of *internal organization* – whether by formal membership; a collective public manifestation such as an exhibition, publication, or manifesto (both

Futurism and Imagism); or a looser group association (the Bloomsbury group). Second, he considers the *external relations* of a group to other groups or to society – whether they specialized in a certain style or medium; where they provided an alternative facility for production, exhibition or publication (Monro's Poetry Bookshop, Imagist anthologies); or cases where the lack of an outlet for alternative views is raised to an active opposition to society and its institutions (Dadaism, Futurism).[32] Using this terminology we can certainly say that in terms of external relations Imagism had little active opposition to existing art institutions, unlike Futurism, which famously decried all museums for being entombed in the past. But in terms of their internal organization the two groups were very similar, even to the extent of the shared authoritarian personalities at their head. Though the Futurists may have presented themselves as a collective, it was clearly Marinetti who dictated the terms of that presentation. Harold Monro, writing in *Poetry and Drama* in June 1913, summed up a similar view of Pound when he described the new movement of Imagism as being 'under the formidable dictatorship of Ezra Pound'.[33]

The nature of Imagism as a cultural formation changed, however, once Pound was no longer its leader. The nature of the dispute between Pound and Lowell has been much documented, although it is only relatively recently that Lowell's role in promoting Imagism, particularly in America, has received full attention. Critics for a long time have accepted at face value Pound's account of the dispute, whereby his 'laconic' and 'objective' Imagist movement declined into Lowell's 'Amygism', which published poetry replete with 'sloppiness, lack of cohesion, lack of organic centre in individual poems, rhetoric'.[34] Later chapters look more closely at these supposed stylistic differences, but here it is revealing to consider how Lowell and Pound quarrelled over the shape of the cultural formation of Imagism itself. At one level the row between the two Americans was intensely personal: the millionairess Lowell and the struggling bohemian poet Pound had similar personalities. Despite sharing a commitment to innovation in verse, both wished to be 'leaders', albeit with different tactics, of a literary movement. Gender clearly played a key part in Pound's feelings and he ridiculed Lowell's size, taking delight in the term Witter

Bynner invented for her, 'the Hippopoetess'.[35] Notoriously, Pound attempted to embarrass her at an Imagist dinner in Dieudonné's restaurant in 1914 by having an old tin bath brought out, a pointed parody of both her body size and her poem 'In a Garden', which referred to a figure bathing. Pound had included Lowell's poem in *Des Imagistes*, but this stunt indicated his rejection of Lowell as an Imagist.[36] Crudely, Pound perceived Lowell as an obese cigar-smoking female poet of doubtful ability who, unfortunately for him, possessed the finances Pound knew were crucial for funding Imagism.

It soon became clear to the other Imagists that the cohabitation of such large personalities was impossible within a single movement, but also that they exhibited differing modes for leading the promotional culture of Imagism and, indeed, for the internal organization of the group. Richard Aldington, H.D., F. S. Flint, John Gould Fletcher, and D. H. Lawrence all opted, for diverse reasons, to join Lowell against Pound when she decided to publish a new Imagist anthology, but one organized on different principles. As Aldington reports it, Lowell desired a number of changes to the formation:

> the immediate abolition of his [Pound's] despotism and the substitution of a pure democracy. There was to be no more of the Duce business, with arbitrary inclusions and exclusions and a capricious censorship. We were to publish quietly and modestly as a little group of friends with similar tendencies, rather than water-tight dogmatic principles. Each poet was to choose for himself what he considered best in his year's output.... To preserve democratic equality names would appear in alphabetical order.[37]

If we trust Aldington's account, it brings Pound's Imagism closer to the 'movement' of Futurism, as characterized by Rainey, while also suggesting that Lowell's Imagism was organized more like a 'school' of equal friends. Pound was invited to contribute but, perhaps not surprisingly given that he felt it was his invention, refused to join a 'democratic beer-garden'.[38] At one level this was because Pound was now busy with the Vorticist movement which he perhaps viewed as a stronger challenger to Futurism, but in another sense the dispute over 'democracy' is a crucial one for understanding the formation of Imagism. Pound had written enthusiastically in an *Egoist* article on Wyndham Lewis that the 'aristocracy of the arts' was now in the ascendancy over the traditional aristocracy of British society.[39] The distinction between an Imagist aristocracy and an Imagist democracy is more than merely terminological, since it indicates how the leader viewed the character of the group, and also how it might present itself to the external world.

The dispute between the two impresarios of Imagism is most forcefully registered in an exchange of letters between Pound and Lowell in the latter part of 1914. Pound felt that his movement was being manoeuvred out of his hands, and even contemplated suing Lowell's for breach of copyright of the term 'Imagiste'. Lowell consulted her brother, who was a lawyer, and then replied to Pound: 'So far as I know you have not copyrighted the name "Imagiste"; I never heard of a school of poetry being copyrighted. I doubt if it could be done.... You would be obliged to prove my inclusion in your group as a libel, and it would interesting to see whether that could be done'.[40] Again this dispute, and its employment of legal discourse, reminds one more of the advertising of rival soaps than the production of poetry. But it does indicate that both parties were highly aware of the value of a marketable image or brand for Imagism. This concern for marketing was not, however, at the expense of the quality of the poetry itself. Writing of the schism between herself and Pound to Harriet Monroe, Lowell noted that Pound's *Des Imagistes* did not sell well, arguing that 'Advertising is all very well but one must have some goods to deliver, and the goods must be up to the advertisement'.[41]

Pound also objected to Lowell's new plans for publishing the anthologies along democratic lines, feeling that he did not want to be constrained by a 'dam'd contentious, probably incompetent committee' and that he would not 'waste time to argue with a committee'.[42] The tension between the individual and the group within a cultural movement is strongly in evidence here. Pound's objection is to how Lowell wished to change the internal organization of the formation: aristocratic artists do not bother with committees. The 1915 Preface to *Some Imagist Poets 1915* made clear the new organization of the group:

> Instead of an arbitrary selection by an editor, each poet has been permitted to represent himself by the work he considers his best....A sort of informal committee – consisting of more than half the authors here represented – have arranged the book and decided

what should be printed and what omitted, but, as a general rule, the poets have been allowed absolute freedom in this direction....Also, to avoid any appearance of precedence, they have been put in alphabetical order. (*SIP 1915* v–vi)

Whether the new arrangement produced a better anthology than Pound's 'arbitrary' editorial choices in *Des Imagistes* is a question of debate. The significant point here is to note how Lowell's actions altered the cultural formation of Imagism, both in its relations between the members and in its external relations to the cultural marketplace of modernism. A more difficult question is to trace how this change in the character of the group had an impact upon the poetry itself.

Lowell's use of the term 'the Imagist School' indicates something of the role she envisaged for the group. In a sense they were to be educators, informing the public of the 'new poetry' by means of the anthologies and related events. Regardless of whether we agree with Pound that Imagism was 'diluted' by Lowell's leadership, it is indisputable that Lowell succeeded in publicizing the group. For Aldington, Pound was the inventor of the Imagist 'movement' and Lowell 'put it across'.[43] Lowell conceded that Pound invented the name 'Imagism', but argued that 'changing the whole public attitude from derision to consideration came from my work'.[44] T. S. Eliot dubbed her the 'demon saleswoman', and indeed Lowell ensured that the public bought the Imagist anthologies, eschewing the notion that modernist verse was only ever an elitist phenomenon.[45] Of the 750 copies printed of the 1915 *Some Imagist Poets*, some 481 were sold in advance; after six months a second edition was printed and overall the volume sold around 1,300 in the first year, figures also achieved by the 1916 anthology.[46] Although they did not sell as well as the Georgian anthologies, the first two Imagist anthologies only went out of print in 1924, and Lowell continued to send small royalties to contributors for a number of years.[47]

Perhaps of more interest than mere sales of the volume, however, were the promotional activities carried out by Lowell for the new 'school'. Writing to her editor at Houghton Mifflin publishers, Lowell noted, 'you have not only an author in me, but an extremely good advertiser. My lectures have been worth more to you than all the advertising in the papers or efforts of salesmen'.[48] Lowell not only arranged the publication of the three anthologies but also promoted Imagism through numerous articles and reviews, flamboyant readings, and extensive lecture tours across America in 1916 and 1917. She even gave perhaps the first reading of modernist verse on radio, on an American station in 1922 (just after the baseball scores).[49] As Jayne Marek comments on Lowell's advertising activities, 'Lowell's energetic promotion of poetry on both commercial and aesthetic grounds is particularly significant because the flux between high and low culture helped bring about literary modernism'.[50] Though Imagism was clearly not a cultural product geared to a mass market, Lowell's promotional work did utilize many of the strategies employed in that cultural field.

Lowell thus sought to make Imagism a poetic product that was read by the public by changing the market for modernism itself. She saw the marketing value of the group identity and also perceived that its organization around democratic principles would ensure that contributors remained on board for the three years of the anthologies. In this way she managed the inevitable tension between individual artist and group identity reasonably successfully. In the crowded marketplace of modernism in the first quarter of the twentieth century Lowell's Imagist 'committee' achieved much success, particularly in America, not by trumpeting Imagism against other movements, like the Vorticists when they tried to dismiss Futurism, but by presenting Imagism as a 'school' that was at the forefront of a wider modern movement.

2

Publishing, Publicity, and Magazines

The acclaimed critic and biographer Richard Ellmann once suggested that 'Literary movements pass their infancy in inarticulate disaffection, but mature when they achieve a vocabulary'.[1] One might add that another marker of successful adulthood for twentieth-century literary movements was the dissemination of this vocabulary in the pages of one or more magazines. The previous chapter examined the pressures that impelled the Imagist movement into being, considering the necessity for modernist poets to group together in order to publicly voice their disaffection. This chapter considers further how Pound and Lowell utilized strategies of advertisement and publicity for Imagism, distributing Imagist ideas as widely as possible across the field of literary publication. Particularly significant was the use of the many modernist little magazines in the period, a fact demonstrated by the publication of Pound's *Des Imagistes* collection in a magazine (*The Glebe*) prior to book publication. Returning Imagist poetry to the periodical presses where it was often first published, first reviewed, and first criticized, presents a more complex picture of how the verse emerged than when we read the poems in later anthologies, like those of Peter Jones, William Pratt or Bob Blaisdell, or in the collected poems of the individual authors. We also read and interpret an Imagist poem quite differently when we encounter it in the pages of a magazine like *The Egoist*, where it jostles for space alongside a serialized novel by Joyce, an editorial on women's rights, or a philosophical consideration of contemporary anarchism. As Peter McDonald argues, asking 'where and how texts were first published... is a way into a much larger series of questions which challenge our understanding of how texts relate to their many, shifting contexts'.[2]

Almost all of the key Imagists wrote, funded or were involved editorially with modernist magazines. In Britain H.D. and Richard Aldington were assistant editors on *The Egoist*; Flint wrote and reviewed widely for *The New Age*, *Poetry and Drama*, and *The Poetry Review*, while Pound wrote for just about every key magazine in the period but with a prominent voice in the American magazines, *Poetry* and *The Little Review*. At various times Fletcher and Lowell were financial supporters for magazines, and Pound in particular understood the importance of having a periodical in which new modernist ideas could be advertised. In America a key publication for Imagism was Harriet Monroe's *Poetry*, started in October 1912 in Chicago, and the place where 'Imagisme' and 'A Few Don'ts by an Imagiste', the earliest manifesto statements of the movement, were published in March 1913. In Britain one of the earliest Imagist poems published was in Monro's *Poetry Review*, where the February 1912 issue printed eight poems by Pound, including one ('$\triangle\Omega$PIA') which was to be reprinted in *Des Imagistes*. Critical commentary upon the contribution of magazines to the Imagist movement has, until recently, been fairly muted. For example, J. B. Harmer's standard history of Imagism, *Victory in Limbo* (1975) contains only three short references to *The Egoist*.

The quintessential character of modernism might be said to exist in the phenomenon of the little magazine. The social and economic pressures on culture that were discussed in the previous chapter are equally relevant for understanding why modernism spawned so many small periodicals. For Pound, such publications were 'free magazines', willing to take experimental work regardless of whether a readership existed for it and with little concern for the commercial gain that might possibly accrue from such ventures. In 1930 Pound argued that

> the history of contemporary letters has, to a very manifest extent, been written in such magazines. The commercial magazines have been content and are still more than content to take derivative products ten or twenty years after the germ has appeared in the free magazines.[3]

The 'value' of such magazines was not financial, since many had tiny circulations, but consisted in getting certain authors into print for the first time. As Pound had indicated to Joyce, there was an 'advertising value' to being published in *The Egoist*, even if only 200 copies on average were sold of each issue. The first critical account of little magazines, from 1947, broadly agreed with Pound's view of their significance. According to Hoffman, Allen, and Ulrich:

> A little magazine is a magazine designed to print artistic work which for reasons of commercial expediency is not acceptable to the money-minded periodicals or presses.... Such periodicals are, therefore, non-commercial by intent.... No doubt little magazine editors would welcome a circulation of a million of two, but they know that their magazines will appeal only to a limited group, generally not more than a thousand persons. And so, financially limited, editors generally caution contributors to banish all thought of remuneration, to be satisfied with payment 'in fame, not specie'.... Coming into use during the First World War, 'little' did not refer to the size of the magazines, nor to their literary contents, nor to the fact that they usually did not pay for contributions. What the word designated.... was a limited group of intelligent readers: to be such a reader one had to understand the aims of the particular schools of literature that the magazines represented, had to be interested in learning about dadaism, vorticism, expressionism, and surrealism.[4]

These two views of the 'little magazine' replicate some of the divisions discussed in the previous chapter – between mass publishing and minority periodicals, between magazines constrained by a commercial agenda and those 'free magazines' which ignored financial considerations as much as possible. However, more recent critical work has again questioned the absolute bifurcation between these forms of periodical. Mark Morrisson's *The Public Face of Modernism* argues that certain modernist magazines often aped the strategies of publicity, advertising, and circulation associated with mainstream publications. Far from wanting only to reach a 'limited group of intelligent readers', as Hoffman et al. suggest, Morrisson asserts that magazines like *The Egoist* were not happy to exist as coterie publications, but rather wished to intervene and help shape a more widely conceived public sphere in which questions of politics and aesthetics were paramount topics for debate.

Modernists sought to adapt the institutions and practices of mass circulation publishing for their own ends, and hoped to make their own voices and opinions heard by a new public seemingly eager to read widely about contemporary culture and society.[5]

To some extent both accounts are accurate – it all depends upon which of the hundreds of modernist magazines one considers.[6] However, in terms of the role played by magazines in the promotion of Imagist poetry, Morrisson's analysis of *The Egoist* as a periodical that employed mass-market strategies of advertising and publicity has much to recommend it. Here I want to focus on three issues in relation to *The Egoist*: the history of the magazine's development and its miscellaneous contents; the machinations of Pound to gain control of a magazine to act as the mouthpiece for the Imagist movement; and, finally, the nature of the Imagist material published in its pages.

The Egoist used to be viewed, in the words of the eminent critic Hugh Kenner, as a magazine 'read chiefly by cranks, feminist and other'.[7] Recent modernist criticism has taken considerably more interest in the cranky parts of the magazine, viewing its discussion of anarchism, homosexuality, and women's rights as forming fascinating parallels and contrasts to the literary and cultural contributions contained in its pages.[8]

The initial predecessor to *The Egoist* was the *The Freewoman*, which began publication in 1911 and was founded by Dora Marsden and Mary Gawthorpe. A typical example of the modern, educated woman who rejected Victorian roles for women, Marsden was a philosophy graduate who had joined, and then fallen out with, the leading women's suffrage group, the Women's Social and Political Union (WSPU). Marsden intended *The Freewoman* as a feminist forum for discussion beyond that authorized by the Pankhursts' autocratic leadership of the WSPU. For Marsden, the call by the WSPU for 'Votes for Women' was too limited a topic for what she perceived as revolutionary times: 'feminism is the whole issue, political enfranchisement a branch issue'.[9] Within the pages of the journal a reader would find Marsden attacking monogamy, advocating a national system of nurseries, and debating the need for free advice upon contraception. Other articles discussed 'auto-eroticism' and homosexuality, and 'Freewoman

Discussion Circles' continued the debates stimulated by the paper. As Morrisson notes, *The Freewoman* attracted an interesting range of advertisements aimed at the apparently newly liberated woman: department stores such as Debenham and Freebody; women's patent medicines; Farrow's Bank for Women; and also for radical bookshops and specialist literary magazines like *Poetry Review*.[10] As Morrisson argues, *The Freewoman* was important to modernist authors for its 'attempt to form a broader and more generally anti-bourgeois oppositional public sphere' that would discuss not only suffragism but anarchism, homosexuality, and radical economic reforms, as well as experimental art and literature.[11] As early as the second issue the magazine included poetry, soon adding short stories, reviews and discussions of contemporary exhibitions such as that by the Futurists at the Sackville Galleries in 1912. This broad alliance between politics and aesthetics was promoted by Rebecca West, co-editor for a short while, who urged Marsden to include literary material: 'I don't see why a movement towards freedom of expression in literature shouldn't be associated with and inspired by your gospel'.[12]

The Freewoman continued until the distributor, W. H. Smith, boycotted the paper in September 1912 because of certain articles which 'render the paper unsuitable to be exposed on the bookstalls for general sale'.[13] Unbowed, Marsden relaunched the magazine in June 1913 as *The New Freewoman: An Individualist Review*, with financial assistance from Harriet Shaw Weaver (who was later to provide similar support to James Joyce) and editorial help from Rebecca West. Individualism now became the key discourse in the magazine, as an advertising flyer made clear: this was the 'only journal of recognised standing espousing a doctrine of philosophic individualism' and it promised to 'lay bare the individualist basis of all that is most significant in modern movements including feminism'.[14] Marsden's philosophical individualism or 'egoism', informed by the anarchist thought of Max Stirner, thus dovetailed smoothly with certain ideas within Imagism. The 1916 Imagist anthology declared the poets to be 'Individualists', and a number of commentators have drawn parallels between Marsden's egoism as a critique of the liberal state, and the intellectual focus upon an aesthetics of individualism in writers such as Pound, T. E. Hulme, and James Joyce.[15]

Another parallel exists between Imagist attacks on poetic rhetoric (considered further in chapter 4) and Marsden's critique of the suffragette movement for employing 'empty concepts' and linguistic abstractions. Marsden argued that the suffragettes, led by Pankhurst, had become 'pinioned with words – words – words' and meaningless concepts such as 'freedom', 'cause' or 'Woman' itself. For Marsden the 'Verbal Age' of 1913 would be routed if 'we recognise that there exists nothing save things and the relations between things'.[16] Rejecting abstract political terms and mistrusting words themselves found many echoes in Imagist theory, as Pound had insisted in the same year that 'the natural object is always the adequate symbol' and that Imagist poetry demonstrated a 'Direct treatment of the "thing", whether subjective or objective'.[17]

Throughout 1913 the contents of *The New Freewoman* gradually shifted emphasis, with articles upon 'Free Love' and 'The Eclipse of Women' being joined by more literary and cultural discussion. Pound wrote to Harriet Monroe, editor of *Poetry*, that he had 'taken charge of the literature dept.' of what he called 'our left wing, *The Freewoman*'.[18] The issue for 1 November contained two articles by Pound, other literary material by Huntley Carter and Allen Upward, a serial story by French author Remy de Gourmont, and adverts for Pound's translation of the medieval poet Arnaut Daniel and for *Poetry* magazine in Chicago. In December of 1913 a letter, signed by three contributors to *Des Imagistes* (Pound, Aldington, and Allen Upward) and three other men, called for the magazine to change its name from being associated with 'an unimportant reform in an obsolete political institution' to a title 'which will mark the character of your paper as an organ of individuals of both sexes and of the individualist principle in every department of life'.[19] Some critics have seen this change of name as a simple androcentric coup engineered by Pound.[20] But Marsden supported the name change at a Director's Meeting in November, possibly as a way of guaranteeing the financial viability of the magazine, which was beginning to struggle, with lower numbers of subscribers and little revenue from advertisements.[21] Marsden, however, also agreed with the change of emphasis from 'feminism' to 'individualism', as it was in keeping with her own intellectual trajectory.

The Egoist: An Individualist Review was thus published on 1 January 1914 and soon became a key mouthpiece for publishing modernism. In particular *The Egoist* was closely identified with the Imagist movement, becoming 'the citadel of Imagism', as a later critic put it.[22] Aldington was now an assistant editor, and the first issue contained some poems by Flint, as well as Wyndham Lewis on Cubism. Poetry by H.D. initially appeared in February (along with serialization of Joyce's *A Portrait of the Artist*), and in the same month Amy Lowell was first included; in March, poems by Fletcher were published. The first visible mention of Imagism as a movement occurs with an article of 1 June by Aldington entitled, 'Modern Poetry and the Imagists', where he restated 'the fundamental doctrines of the group' in relation to style and technique, illustrating the article with poems by H.D. ('Hermes of the Ways'), Pound ('Liu Ch'e') and Flint ('Hallucination'). The article can clearly be read as part of a concerted strategy by Pound to promote Imagism as a movement in a magazine over which he, and the other Imagists, now exercised considerable control. All three poems discussed by Aldington were included in *Des Imagistes,* which had been recently published in *The Glebe*, and in book form in London in April. Another element in the publicizing of the magazine and Imagism was the use of advertisements. Fletcher recalled that during the spring of 1914 'the paper went so far as to have flaming contents bills displayed at Charing Cross and other places in London'. Aldington also arranged for sandwichboard men to patrol the streets in May 1914, displaying the contents of *The Egoist*.[23]

A further strategy in the promotion of Imagism in *The Egoist* was to publish the same work in other little magazines. For example, two of the four poems by Flint that were published in the first issue of *The Egoist* had been published in *Poetry* the year before. In February the same technique was used with H.D.'s poetry while, in the 1 June issue, Pound published an article on *Poetry* magazine, under the impressively preposterous pseudonym Bastien von Helmholtz. *Poetry*, he declared, 'prints more important poems than all the rest of the American magazines put together'.[24] Pound, of course, did not add that he had submitted much of this work, or that it could also be viewed in the pages of *The Egoist*. Such strategies of logrolling or mutual marketing across various magazines show just how crucial magazines were in the dissemination of a new literary movement.

Pound's perception of the vital role that a literary magazine could play in promoting the Imagist movement is also apparent in the negotiations between himself, Amy Lowell, and John Gould Fletcher in 1913–14. Pound was to write in 1914 that although great art did not depend on 'the support of riches...without such aid it will be individual, separate and spasmodic; it will not group and become a great period...a great age means the deliberate fostering of genius, the gathering-in and grouping and encouragement of artists'.[25] Over the decades this was to become a familiar mantra from Pound, but even at this early stage of his career he understood the worth of acquiring a well-funded literary magazine in which to foster the modernist cause. Not long after Pound was introduced to Fletcher in Paris, some time in April 1913, Pound suggested that Fletcher provide financial support for *The New Freewoman*. Fletcher, financially independent after the death of his father, had published five books of poems at his own expense in 1913 and had harboured ideas of founding a literary review. Some time earlier he had learnt of the financial difficulties besetting Ford Madox Ford's *English Review* and had sought to buy it, 'feeling that the proprietorship of so distinguished a periodical would be the best means of establishing my name and reputation among the literary circles of London'. Two years later, and with several volumes of poetry published, Fletcher expressed rather more altruistic motives: 'I now felt my money was of no further use to me except as a means of helping other struggling young authors to find an outlet for their work'.[26] Upon learning of Fletcher's ideas Pound proposed that he fund *The New Freewoman*. Fletcher agreed, with the proviso that he did not want his own work to appear or be praised in the magazine by Pound. However, Pound did review favourably Fletcher's poetry in *The New Freewoman*. Annoyed, Fletcher wrote to Amy Lowell explaining what had happened, stating that he was withdrawing funding from the paper, and urging Lowell not to let her poems be included in Pound's forthcoming anthology.[27]

Fletcher's protest might be considered rather precious, given that only two years earlier he had thought of buying a periodical to establish his name in literary circles. However, Fletcher's comments underline the importance of periodical publication for new literary movements, even though he personally expresses repugnance at the tactic:

> That is the 'artistic' 'literary' life as it is lived in London today. A lot of tradesmen puffing each other's wares would be a better name for them. I do not call such people artists. I call them dealers in self-advertisement.... Of all things on Earth, the most nauseating, the most abominable, is the London literary clique with its external politeness and internal petty jealousies and underground tactics .... I prefer the low admiration of the vulgar, or the cold contempt of all, to that sort of admiration which can only be bought with favours, to the P. T. Barnum methods of advertising that are in vogue in this twentieth century of commercialized 'art' and 'book-markets'.[28]

Fletcher's focus upon how commerce and advertising taint the production of art echoes the kind of complaint made by Gissing's character Reardon, in *New Grub Street*. As a consequence of this, and other objections, Fletcher did not allow Pound to include his work in *Des Imagistes*. However, by April 1914 Fletcher's principled objections seemed to have receded and he had patched up his differences with Pound. This is shown in an anecdote about Fletcher sending Pound a poem, 'Blue Symphony', which Pound placed with *Poetry* magazine. Fletcher recalled that he received $100 for the poem, the most he had been paid for his verse: all of it, he noted ruefully, went 'to paying Pound's own contributors to *The Egoist*'.[29] The story suggests that although Fletcher found the London literary marketplace 'nauseating', he was unable to resist its allures absolutely.

While Fletcher found the activities of a literary 'tradesman' objectionable, Pound was happy to play such a role for Imagism in relation to *The Egoist* magazine. Finding that Fletcher was not willing to bankroll the magazine, Pound turned to Lowell for money. Early in 1914 he wrote to Lowell asking, 'Do you want to edit *The Egoist*?'[30] Pound claimed that Marsden had written to him saying that she was willing to quit, but that the magazine would need financial support as it was only assured until June. With 'any sort of business management the thing ought to pay its expenses', remarked Pound, also suggesting that Aldington be paid more in order to take increased editorial responsibilities and that 'the sex problem' discussed in the paper would need to be dropped. Clearly interested in this offer, although perhaps wary after Fletcher's warning to her, Lowell wrote back to Pound requiring more information about editorial policies and whether the paper could be transferred in some fashion to Boston, where she lived. Towards the end of March Pound wrote to Lowell that *The Egoist* had just received £250 (possibly now from Fletcher) and so 'there's no chance of your getting it in July to do as *you* like with'. As an alternative, Pound suggested that Lowell start a quarterly publication, rather than the fortnightly *Egoist*, that she could edit in Boston and with a London staff that Pound could provide:

> Hueffer [Ford], Joyce, Lawrence, Flint, and myself on this side and you and your crowd on the other. I should also develop some more intimate connection with Vienna and Florence. We could have whoever we liked for special articles or stories, but I think Lawrence and Joyce are the two strongest prose writers among les jeunes ....And we could have anything Yeats happened to do.[31]

Pound's overtures to Lowell about such a publication again indicate how both characters considered carefully the mechanics of getting Imagism into print. Pound's plan to get Lowell to edit *The Egoist* was, however, far from innocent. He later wrote to Margaret Anderson, editor of the American magazine *The Little Review* about Anderson's proposal to publish Lowell in *The Little Review*: 'Re/Amy. I DON'T want her. But if she can be made to liquidate, to excoriate, to cash in, on a magazine THEN would I be right glad to see her milked of her money, mashed into moonshine, at mercy of monitors'.[32] Pound clearly viewed Lowell primarily as a patron, rather than a poet, of Imagism, and thought that her funding of a magazine – whether *The Egoist* or a new publication – would fulfil the 'fostering of genius' that Pound believed was necessary for a great period of art.

Lowell, not surprisingly, had different views on her role in Imagism, but perhaps agreed with Pound that modernist writing had to engage with the marketplace so despised by someone like Fletcher. Lowell's sense that Imagist poetry should present itself as analogous to a business suited a woman who once said of herself: 'I made myself a poet, but the Lord made me a business man'.[33] Like any good 'business man' Lowell was careful not to throw her money into projects that would not succeed and she was cautious about funding a periodical like *The Egoist*. Lowell wrote that Pound 'was anxious for me to run an international review' and that she would 'guarantee all the money, and put in what I pleased, and he was to run the magazine his way. We talked over the cost of expenses, and we both thought that $5000 a year was the least that such a magazine could be run on'. When Lowell informed Pound that she did not have this amount to hand, Pound, she says, lost his temper and 'accused me of being unwilling to give any money towards art'.[34] According to Jayne Marek, Lowell realized that publishing Imagism in a number of anthologies would 'create the effect of a literary review' and it was this strategy she adopted over that of gaining control of a magazine.[35] Lowell also sought to get Imagism published in more mainstream literary magazines, such as the conservative *Atlantic Monthly*, badgering the editor, Ellery Sedgwick, to accept poetry from Lawrence and other new poets.[36]

Lowell's efforts in arranging for the three anthologies of Imagism to appear indicate her commitment to enabling new art, contrary to Pound's accusation. Lowell secured the well-established Houghton Mifflin to publish the anthologies, after Macmillan had refused the volume because of threatened litigation from Pound over use of the Imagist name. The schism with Pound, however, meant there was some debate among the Imagists over what to call the new volume and a variety of peculiar names were proposed: 'The Six', 'The Allies', 'The Independents', 'The Vitalists', 'The Young American Club' and 'The Quintessentialists'. Flint rejected all of these and argued that the group had best stick to 'the old title of Some Imagists or whatever it was. Never mind about Ezra. He no more invented Imagism than he invented the moon'.[37] Ferris Greenslet, the editor at Houghton Mifflin, also wanted to keep the name for its 'mercantile value' and so the group of Aldington, Fletcher, Flint, H.D., Lawrence, and Lowell agreed upon *Some Imagist Poets 1915*. It was a clearer designation than the faux French 'Imagiste', and the use of 'some' left open the idea that there were other poets practising Imagism who just happened not to be included.

Although Lowell's efforts now turned to overseeing the publication of the anthologies, she also continued to utilize little magazines for the Imagist cause. In May 1915 she and Fletcher wrote a review of *Some Imagist Poets* under the pseudonym George Lane, for *The Little Review*.[38] Also in May came the special Imagist number of *The Egoist*, and Lowell had organized for a number of copies of this particular issue to be sent to her for distribution in America. However, Lowell disliked certain of the contents (Harold Monro's piece in particular) for offering measured assessments of Imagism rather than the uncritical 'puffing' and 'log-rolling' she thought the movement required at this stage. Annoyed at what she saw as a failure to advertise Imagism properly, Lowell did not distribute the copies of *The Egoist*, keeping them and paying for each copy.

When we view this special Imagist issue we might think that Lowell's disapproval was rather misjudged. The issue did much to highlight and praise the Imagists, and Aldington noted how *Egoist* subscriptions increased soon after the special issue was published.[39] The issue included very little adverse criticism (aside from Monro's reticent praise for the group), and was almost entirely written by the Imagists themselves: Aldington wrote on Flint and Pound; Flint wrote on H.D.; Fletcher wrote on Lowell. Ferris Greenslet, the editor at Houghton Mifflin who was bringing out *Some Imagist Poets 1915*, also discussed Fletcher's poetry. An outsider might well have found agreement with Fletcher's earlier criticism of such examples of cultural self-advertisement: 'That is the "artistic" "literary" life as it is lived in London today. A lot of tradesmen puffing each other's wares would be a better name for them'. The issue represented the culmination of over a year of publishing Imagist verse in *The Egoist*, with almost every issue containing poems by Flint, Fletcher, Aldington, H.D., or Lowell. Pound's criticism kept appearing, but not his verse. The publicity campaign was also continued after the special issue, with Aldington writing an article on Lowell in July 1914, and then, rather oddly, woodcut images of Aldington and Fletcher appeared in October and November. H.D. became assistant editor with Aldington in December 1914, roles the two kept until T. S. Eliot took over in June 1917. Only now did Imagist poetry stop appearing in the magazine, coinciding with the last of the anthologies. *The Egoist* continued until 1919, publishing extracts from Joyce's *Ulysses* and Wyndham Lewis's *Tarr*, but suffering from low circulations (it averaged only 200 sales from 1916 to 1919).

Viewing the pages of *The New Freewoman* and *The Egoist* in these years we see a fascinating confluence of different discourses within modernity and modernism. Marsden's 'lingual psychology' and critique of the 'science of signs' replaced the earlier discussions of sexuality and feminism instigated in *The Freewoman*. Her article 'Women's Rights' in October 1914 signalled this change of direction starkly: 'The War... has brought the wordy contest about Women's Rights to an abrupt finish, and only a few sympathetic words remain to be spoken over the feminist corpse'.[40] *The Egoist* was now home to a different critique of language, with many key modernist writers and texts being first published here. The Imagist group exerted an even stronger hold on the magazine and, although neither Pound nor Lowell gained complete control, the editorial direction of Aldington, H.D., and Pound meant that *The Egoist* can rightly be described as the 'house journal' of Imagism. Not only did it give valuable space to Imagist poetry, but it also allowed critical articles that expounded the ideas and theories behind the new verse. The next chapter turns to this important dimension of the Imagist movement, and considers many of the prose statements that accompanied the appearance of Imagist poetry in little magazines such as *The Egoist* and *Poetry*.

3

Prefaces and Manifestos

The symbiotic relationship between the Imagist movement and the many little magazines that emerged in modernism is evident in the prose publications written to announce the work of the group. To the key articles, 'Imagisme' and 'A Few Don'ts by an Imagiste', published in *Poetry* (Chicago) in March 1913, can be added many of the critical articles from *The Egoist*, the prefaces from *Some Imagist Poets*, and other texts by Amy Lowell, T. E. Hulme, and May Sinclair. The multiple prose discussions of Imagism are worth considering for a number of reasons: first, following the tenor of the argument in the previous two chapters, to understand how such texts functioned as part of the advertising and publicity strategies of the Imagist movement; second, to consider how these forms of Imagist theory related to Imagist practice, and whether a failure to follow Imagist 'rules' in the poems made any difference whatsoever.

The two texts published in *Poetry*, 'Imagisme' and 'A Few Don'ts by an Imagiste', can be considered the nearest document to a manifesto of Imagism. They announced Imagism to a reading public, and Pound was fond of referring to them in later critical writings.[1] Interestingly, 'A Few Don'ts' was intended to accompany rejection slips sent out by *Poetry*, indicating the close link between the discourse of magazine publication and the Imagists.[2] It also suggests that the document was not directly a manifesto, or at least was a text that could be adapted for different purposes. Imagism's ambiguous use of the manifesto format seems to place it as a cultural formation somewhere between the Georgian poets and the Futurist group. The first Georgian anthology contained a prefatory note, written by Edward Marsh, which modestly claimed the volume was issued 'in the belief that English poetry is now once again putting on a new strength and beauty'. No sense of a collective entity called the Georgians is in evidence, with the name being referred to merely as 'another "Georgian period" which may take rank in due time with the several great poetic ages of the past'.[3] The Futurists, however, had trumpeted their arrival in a number of manifestos, from 1909 onwards, including manifestos for sculpture, music, and 1913's 'Futurist Manifesto of Lust'. Futurism clearly proclaimed itself as a movement and stated emphatically what it stood for: 'We intend to sing the love of danger, the habit of energy and fearlessness....We affirm that the world's magnificence has been enriched by a new beauty: the beauty of speed'.[4] The Futurists proclaimed themselves as a young movement with a rhetoric of violence and destruction designed to shock and outrage the public.

Between these two extremes, Imagism emerged. Wyndham Lewis, the founder of Vorticism and the nearest cultural formation in tone and stance to that of Futurism, argued that in 1914, 'If you were in a movement you were expected to shout. One was surrounded – one was hemmed-in – by mob-orators'.[5] If the Futurists continued to shout loudly, and the Georgians merely whispered their presence to the world (although their anthology sold massively), the Imagists seemed caught between these two modes of announcing one's arrival on the literary scene.

Tracing the manifesto as a form of writing, Janet Lyon notes how the political discourse of the manifesto was transferred into the aesthetic discourse of modernism:

> In the decades following the revolutionary activities of the 1871 Commune, the manifesto emerged as the signature genre for avant-garde groups announcing the birth of artistic movements. The aesthetic coteries of the historical avant-garde – from symbolists to vorticists, from futurists to surrealists – adapted the manifesto's revolutionary discourse to signal their own radical departures from bourgeois artistic forms and practices.[6]

In Britain during the period 1909–19 the revolutionary discourses of political factions such as the suffragettes and the labour movement coincided with the many formations of the aesthetic avant-garde. The use of the manifesto format, notes Lyon, was common to both tendencies and was borrowed or adapted by groups such as the Vorticists to express aesthetic views that occluded the political impetus behind groups such as the suffragettes.

However, when Lyon turns to the Imagists, she argues that the essays 'Imagisme' and 'A Few Don'ts' were forms of 'anti-manifesto'.[7] Lyon asserts that, although these tracts appear similar to Marinetti's manifestos, they differ in that the Imagist texts do not really announce the existence of a new movement or school: 'As several historians of modernism have argued... imagism was more a historical fiction than a relatively real school like vorticism; imagism's 'creation' occurred in a brief and cryptic series of texts designed to advertise Pound's own explicit proposals for the improvement of contemporary (...) poetry'.[8] Lyon thus finds it odd that the other Imagists are not named and that 'Imagisme' uses the impersonal 'they' rather than the pronoun 'we', a grammatical strategy which, for her, defines true manifestos. For Lyon this suggests a coterie closed to other members, unlike the role of a manifesto in recruiting new followers. The texts are more a 'credo' than a manifesto and effect 'a shrinkage of avant-garde goals while sustaining an illusion of avant-garde kinship and familiarity'.[9]

Lyon's argument, however, mistakes a number of key features in these founding documents of Imagism. True, they do not use the tone employed by the Futurists to proclaim a movement akin to a political party, but the 'credo' did function as a form of manifesto statement, both for the public and for other Imagists. John Gould Fletcher, for example, disagreed intensely with the prescriptive nature of Pound's 'rules', as he explained to the editor of *Poetry*: 'I agree with schools only in the French sense, that a "school" represents a certain attitude toward life held in common by a certain group. I do not agree that a poem must be written according to certain fixed rules.... I have informed Mr. Pound that I do not intend to hamper myself with his techniques and his "don'ts."'[10] Fletcher's complaint demonstrates how other poets did view Pound's text as a manifesto, prescribing the rules of a particular school of writing much as a political party might lay out its policy in a manifesto. In 1927, writing to the author of the first critical work on Imagism, Glenn Hughes, Pound would refer to 'Imagisme' as the 'first manifesto' of the movement.[11]

Lyon's point about the pronoun usage in 'Imagisme' also fails to take note of the composition of the piece. The use of 'they' and not 'we' is a function of the illusion of reportage created by Flint and Pound in this essay. Famously Pound had turned up at Flint's house with a text Pound himself had composed and which purported to be that of an interview with Pound, the founder of Imagism. Pound wanted Flint simply to sign the text. However, Flint insisted on editing the 'interview' and so eventually it was published as Flint's interview with an anonymous 'imagiste' poet. Flint was already well known as a reviewer of poetry for *The New Age* and *Poetry Review*, so using him as a respected literary journalist was a rhetorical device by Pound, and the use of 'they' rather than 'we' simply corresponds to the illusion of a journalist interviewing a member of a group. That Flint's knowledge of *vers libre* was crucial for Imagist experimentation and that he too would appear in *Des Imagistes* did not matter: as Pound himself noted, he asked Flint to write a note on Imagism since 'I can't very well do it myself and he is getting known for his knowledge of contemporary work in France so I thought him the best person to describe the school'.[12] Pound clearly believed the 'school' of Imagism existed and thus, contra Lyon, required something like a manifesto to proclaim its existence to the world. Using Flint only typified the strategies of mutual advertising and logrolling in London's literary world that were so bemoaned by Fletcher. The sense of a collective entity called the Imagists had, in any case, already been announced by Pound early in 1912 when he referred to *Les Imagistes*, 'descendants of the forgotten school of 1909'.[13] This group identity was further demonstrated in the opening paragraph of 'A Few Don'ts', where Pound refers to a 'we' and 'our' in the application of the term 'image'.

'Imagisme', then, is a rather curious document that functions as a manifesto, even in the act of disavowing some of the features of the form. This ambiguity is shown in the claim that the 'imagistes' are said to be 'contemporaries of the Post Impressionists and the Futurists', but display 'nothing in common with these schools'. This distinction is glossed by saying that they 'had not published a manifesto. They were not a revolutionary school', but sought only to 'write in accordance with the best tradition'. Pound and Flint recognized that being in a movement was an essential part of the modernist landscape at this point, but they were also aware that a new group must mark out their position as distinct from other formations; hence the rejection of the description of being 'revolutionary', a term self-proclaimed by the Futurists and used by many critics about the 1910 Post-Impressionist Exhibition in London.[14] The use of the term 'tradition' was, in many ways, a clever one, since it distinguished the group from the Futurists, who had called for the destruction of all that was traditional, including museums and libraries, but also encroached upon the territory of the Georgians, whose use of traditional poetic forms had proved to be extremely successful. Imagist poetry was to strike readers as revolutionary, but 'Imagisme' seeks to refute the alarming connotations of this term by embracing its opposite, 'tradition'. 'Imagisme' thus does not, as Lyon argues, create the illusion of being avant-garde, but instead attempts to position carefully the group as a modernist cultural formation, distinct from the self-effacing Georgians and from the 'revolutionary' nature of Futurism. In saying that they had not published a manifesto, the group again distinguished themselves from the manifesto-frenzy of the Futurists. Slyly, they refused to call 'Imagisme' a manifesto, but it clearly functioned as one, with the statement of the 'rules' for Imagist production marking their group identity in a way never considered by the Georgians.

The three Imagist precepts were as follows:

1 Direct treatment of the 'thing', whether subjective or objective.
2 To use absolutely no word that did not contribute to the presentation.
3 As regarding rhythm: to compose in sequence of the musical phrase, not in sequence of a metronome. (*IP* 129)

The article added that there was also a 'Doctrine of the Image', which was unwritten since, if seen by the public, it would only provoke 'useless discussion'. This claim is, by turns, teasing and disingenuous: in refusing to explain the core term of the Imagist name the article creates a sense of mystery around a shared poetic technique (arguably another anti-manifesto feature); the claim was also dissembling in that there already existed several explicit comments upon the role of the 'image' in poetry – arguments made not by Pound, but by Flint and, more significantly, T. E. Hulme. To understand the first two Imagist rules it is necessary to consider, briefly, the impact of the ideas of Hulme. Flint, in his premature history of the movement published in the Imagist issue of *The Egoist,* noted in terms that echo those of 'Imagisme': 'Hulme was the ringleader. He... insisted on absolutely accurate presentation and no verbiage'.[15] Flint later stated that Pound invented the new movement by 'taking the Image from T. E. Hulme' and the ism from Flint's influential article on French poetry for *The Poetry Review* in August 1912.[16] And Pound, even though he thought Flint's history 'bullshit' and tried at times to play down Hulme's influence in favour of Ford Madox Ford's, stated in 1917 that the word 'Imagist' was invented 'on a Hulme basis'.[17]

Pound had first met Hulme in 1909 at the Poets' Club that met at the Tour Eiffel restaurant in London's Soho. Pound also attended a number of lectures given by Hulme in the following years, including those in 1911 on Bergson, who in this period was a major influence on Hulme's thought. These lectures focus often on the nature of language and the idea that poetry is a visual and concrete language that cuts through the abstractions of prose. It was a point Hulme had earlier made in an influential lecture of 1908 on modern poetry, where he argued that poetry was a more direct language than prose, 'direct because it deals in images' (*SW* 64). The first rule in 'Imagisme', relating to the direct treatment of the thing, has a very Hulmean feel to it, particularly in that reference to a subjective or objective 'thing'. Many of Hulme's essays are riven through with an obsession with *things.* As he put it bluntly in his 'Notes on Language and Style': 'Dead things not men as the material for art' (*SW* 41). Hulme argued that poetic language captured this materiality more than other forms of discourse, since poetry can 'Transfer [the] physical to language', and is able to preserve 'an entirely physical thing, a real clay before me... an image'. For Hulme, a word 'is a board with an image or statue on it'; when he speaks in prose all that passes is the board, and the 'statue remains in my imagination' (*SW* 41). Only in poetry can the visual and the physical, the statue, be communicated and it is not surprising that Hulme and others often compared Imagist poems to forms of sculpture.

Public language, argued Hulme, was reliant for its continuation upon the poet: 'Poetry [is] always the advance guard of language' (*SW* 41), since 'plain speech is essentially inaccurate. It is only by new metaphors... that it can be made precise' (*FS* 81). When metaphors are no longer new they become an abstract discourse, since 'abstract words are merely codified dead metaphors' (*FS* 11).[18] Poetry epitomizes a language which resists abstraction through its creation of metaphors, a task assisted by the visual dimension of metaphor: 'every word in the language originates as a live metaphor, but gradually of course all visual meaning goes out of them and they become a kind of counter. Prose is in fact the museum where the dead metaphors of the poets are preserved' (*S* 152). A 'counter' language is Hulme's term for abstract forms of language, and also suggests a modern, reified rationality of mathematics or money. Poetry is not a 'counter' language but is rooted in the 'visual meanings' of metaphor; for the poet, 'Each word must be an image seen, not a counter' (*SW* 38). Images are valued since 'Thought is prior to language and consists in the simultaneous presentation to the mind of two different images' (*SW* 43); language is therefore at something of a remove from this source and, notes Hulme, 'We replace meaning (i.e. vision) with words' (*SW* 37).

This theory of visual meaning was very significant for the development of Imagist aesthetics, and derives from Hulme's reading in nineteenth-century French philosophers, such as Theodule Ribot, Hyppolite Taine, and most importantly, Bergson.[19] In Bergson's *Introduction à la métaphysique*, translated by Hulme in 1913, Bergson asserts that 'the Image has at least this advantage, that it keeps us in the concrete'.[20] In 'Bergson's Theory of Art' Hulme claims that the French philosopher shows reality to be 'a flux of interpenetrated elements unseized by the intellect' (*S* 146). The intellect is an analytic faculty capable only of understanding the world in terms of conceptual abstractions. Reality can only be grasped by intuition, a faculty of concrete experience that bursts through the ever-changing surface appearances of objects to capture their 'real duration' (*durée réelle*). Bergson's model, which rejects surface for depth, and in which formal intellect is ousted by sensual intuition, is echoed in the Imagist call for a 'direct treatment of the thing'.

Hulme's argument recalls Raymond Williams's characterization of a significant view of language held by many modernists: everyday language is seen as a blockage to some true underlying consciousness or state of feeling, and literature must seek to break through these restrictive barriers through new modes of expression.[21] Hulme's particular vision of this quest was to focus upon poetic language in an attempt to show that 'beauty may be in small, dry things' (S 131). Much of Hulme's own poetry, though never included in any of the Imagist anthologies, typified this aesthetic of 'small, dry things', with a fine example being 'Above the Dock':

> Above the quiet dock in midnight,
> Tangled in the tall mast's corded height,
> Hangs the moon. What seemed so far away
> Is but a child's balloon, forgotten after play.

(SW 2)

This poem focuses upon a single visual image, with only the reference to 'quiet' not being a visual descriptor. The directness of the images is conveyed by the simple diction, with only one word ('forgotten') being more than two syllables. The 'thing' being realized is, in a way, both subjective and objective. At one level, the 'thing' is merely a balloon caught up in the mast of a ship, but the poem also records a subjective dimension, both that of the perceiver, who mistook the balloon for the moon and so has confused a near object with that of a distant one, and possibly also that of the child who has discarded it after play has finished. The child that has left the balloon after presumably holding it close echoes the mistake of the person who has perceived the balloon as a distant moon: in one case an object which was far is now near, in the other the nearby object is now far away. This imagery of distance is, of course, very visual and objective, but also suggests a subjective experience of loss or possibly abandonment. Cleverly, the poem points to these subjective intuitions without any pronoun reference or indication of a perceiving consciousness.

The poem's directness is not only the effect of its use of visual concrete images, but also because it 'use[s] absolutely no word that did not contribute to the presentation', as the second rule in 'Imagisme' stated. In 'A Few Don'ts' Pound repeated this guideline: 'Use no superfluous word, no adjective, which does not reveal something' (IP 131). A game that can always be played with Imagist poetry is to check whether this rule has been adhered to, or whether further concision, particularly with adjectival use, is possible without loss of poetic effect. Arguably, the adjective 'quiet' in the first line of 'Above the Dock' could be jettisoned for not revealing something and for being non-visual, although it does convey a sense of detachment from other human beings who might have been at work in the dock or on the ship: attention is thus focused upon the object itself. A much clearer case of where an Imagist has followed this rule to good effect can be found in H.D.'s enigmatic poem 'The Pool'. When first published in *Poetry* it appeared thus:

> Are you alive?
> I touch you with my thumb.
> You quiver like a sea-fish.
> I cover you with my net.
> What are you – banded-one?[22]

But when republished in *Some Imagist Poets 1915* the second line was amended simply to 'I touch you'. H.D. clearly realized that the reference to the thumb was an instance of superfluity, and that, far from revealing something, it actually detracts from the complex relationship between the I and the You in the poem by suggesting only a physical touch by the hand, rather than the possibility of a more metaphysical contact.

Pound later said that the second rule was the keystone of the Imagist programme and although it is often interpreted purely in terms of a call for concision it is worth considering what might be meant by the notion of 'presentation'.[23] At one level it re-emphasizes the notion of a direct treatment of the thing, since it calls for *presentation* and not *representation*. This, however, is a rather puzzling statement in itself, since Imagist poems were just that, poems, made of words, and not of physical things. In 'A Few Don'ts' Pound glosses the notion of presentation as being a poetry that is against abstraction, rhetoric and description. Pound quotes a line of Shakespeare to demonstrate writing which contains 'nothing that one can call description; he presents'. Dante is also praised for a 'definiteness of... presentation, as compared with Milton's rhetoric'. An example of what to avoid is the expression 'dim land *of peace*', writes Pound, which 'dulls the image. It mixes an abstraction with the concrete. It comes from the writer's not realizing that the natural object is always the *adequate* symbol' (*IP* 131). For Pound the 'dim land' is the natural object that could indicate the idea of peace, without the reference to the abstract concept of 'peace'. It is puzzling advice, however, since we might doubt whether all readers could grasp the implied reference to peace in such a 'natural object' as the land.

Desiring an immediate presentation of objects did, however, mark Imagism out as distinct from Symbolist poetry, associated with poets and critics of the 1890s such as Arthur Symons and other members of the Rhymers' Club. It was also intended to distance the Imagists from Victorian verse, and thus to present them as a movement committed to being modern just as much as the Futurists. The novelist and poet May Sinclair, in an article published in the Imagist issue of *The Egoist*, produced an intriguing analogy to elucidate the idea of presentation:

> It (the image) may be either the form of a thing – you will get Imagist poems which are as near as possible to the naked presentation of a thing.... or the Image may be the form of a passion, an emotion or a mood.... The point is that the passion, the emotion, or the mood is never given as an abstraction. And in no case is the Image a symbol of reality (the object); it is reality (the object) itself. You cannot distinguish between the thing and its image.
>
> What the Imagists are 'out for' is direct contact with reality....There must be nothing between you and your object....The Victorian poets are protestant. For them the bread and wine are symbols of Reality...The Imagists are Catholic; they believe in Trans-Substantiation. For them the bread and wine are the body and blood.[24]

For Sinclair the Image is not a symbol, abstracted from actual objects, but is rather a presented thing, a version of Hulme's desire for a poetry to hand over sensations physically, what he called a 'body poetry'.[25] Ultimately, of course, this theory is something of an impossibility, since between a poet and their object will always come the medium of language. This distrust of the very medium in which they practice has lead one critic to suggest that 'Imagism is a self-destructive, an anti-poetic poetics' since it appears to favour things over words.[26] There is some truth in this, although another strategy, discussed in the next chapter, is to seek to reform words to become more like the things to which they refer. This is summed up, inevitably, in a claim made by Pound in a letter to the editor of *Poetry* magazine:

'Language is made out of concrete things'.[27]

The final tenet of 'Imagisme' is more concerned with poetic technique than the philosophy of language. 'As regarding rhythm: to compose in sequence of the musical phrase, not in sequence of a metronome' situated Imagism within debates about *vers libre* (free verse) that Flint and others had introduced into English poetic circles from their reading in French poetry.[28] In H.D.'s 'The Pool', for example, there is neither rhyme nor conventional metre, but a certain musicality is evident in the echoes between the words 'alive', 'quiver', and 'cover'. Arguably, since much Imagist verse was so short the repetitive nature of a repeated rhyme or metrical pattern is never established. Hulme's 'Above the Dock', for example, although it uses a standard AA, BB rhyme scheme can hardly be accused, in just four lines, of exhibiting the properties of a metronome. And the internal rhyme ('moon', 'balloon') and mid-line caesura in lines 3 and 4 stress a sense of the 'musical phrase'. In 'A Few Don'ts' Pound recommended: 'Don't chop you stuff into separate *iambs*. Don't make each line stop dead at the end, and then begin every next line with a heave'. It was this aspect of Imagism, its espousal of a free verse that rejected the metrical forms that had dominated English poetry for centuries, that caught the attention of hostile critics but which also embedded its significance within modernism. As Pound was later to note, getting rid of the pentameter was the first major breakthrough for modernist verse, and Imagism's commitment to such experimentation can be found throughout its verse, from Pound's translations of Japanese and Chinese verse to the 'polyphonic prose' of Lowell and Fletcher.

Often considerations of Imagist theory remain fixated upon these two early manifestos by Pound, but this chapter concludes by discussing some of the remarks found in the prefaces of the 1915 and 1916 anthologies, to detect how the Imagists theorized their work once Pound had left. Pound's 'A Few Don'ts' was followed by the publication a year later of *Des Imagistes*, which contained no prefatory statement. Pound obviously felt that he had done enough proselytizing and would let the poetry stand alone. The reaction to *Des Imagistes* was poor, with some buyers in London sending their copies back.[29] Lowell therefore decided that a preface was necessary for the next anthology and explained this rationale in the preface:

> As it has been suggested that much of the misunderstanding of the former volume was due to the fact that we did not explain ourselves in a preface, we have thought it wise to tell the public what our aims are, and why we are banded together between one set of covers. (*SIP* Preface)

Arguably, this statement contradicts the 'present, don't describe' rhetoric found in Pound's manifestos of 1913, but it also indicates Lowell's awareness that promotion of a new movement required less cryptic forms of justification. It also helped mark out post-Poundian Imagism. Fletcher had wanted a much stronger statement to distinguish the group from Pound, suggesting that the new group write a manifesto entitled 'Against Poundism' as a preface.[30] This did not happen, although a reference to Pound did exist in an early version of the preface which seems to have been drafted by Aldington and then revised by Lowell.[31]

Although the 1915 preface refers to 'Differences of taste and judgement' that have appeared amongst the contributors, prima facie very little distinguished the aesthetic principles of the 1915 volume from the ideas proclaimed in 'A Few Don'ts'. New rhythms are called for, not necessarily a poetry of 'free-verse'. The poet should 'present an image (hence the name: Imagist)' that should 'render particulars exactly and not deal in vague generalities'. Poems should be concentrated, 'hard and clear, never blurred nor indefinite' (*SIP 1915* Preface). In a partial distancing from Hulme's views, the preface argues that poets should 'use the language of common speech', though this is qualified by the call 'to employ always the *exact* word'. This is perhaps the first reference to 'common speech' by the Imagists, although Pound also espoused a similar point of view, writing to Harriet Monroe early in 1915 that poetic language must depart 'in no way from speech save by a heightened intensity (i.e. simplicity)', a view he credited to the influence of Ford Madox Ford.[32]

The 1915 preface is much closer to the rhetorical form normally found in manifestos: the six 'common principles' of this school of poets are more explicit; the formation of the group is explored further, as are the selection principles used by the 'informal committee' so detested by Pound. There is also a more inclusive tone when the preface states that the Imagists are not 'a clique' or 'exclusive artistic sect' but simply wish to establish 'a place for ourselves and our principles'. One can imagine other poets, reading this, believing that they too could become Imagists.

The preface to the 1916 anthology was drafted by Fletcher and probably revised by Lowell.[33] Again the text starts by exploring the need to explain Imagist tenets more comprehensively: 'the very brevity we employed [in *SIP*] has led to a great deal of misunderstanding. We have decided, therefore, to explain the laws which govern us a little more clearly' (*SIP 1916* Preface). The shift from 'rules' ('Imagisme') or 'principles' (*SIP*) to 'laws' is all the more striking given Fletcher's earlier dislike of being hampered by such dictates. It perhaps indicates that a more established sense of the group's identity had been solidified by 1916. A keener sense of Imagism as part of a wider modernist movement that is perceived by the public as 'anarchic and strange' is also now evident. Imagism is part of 'a changed idiom in literature' that asks to be judged by 'different standards than those employed in Nineteenth-Century art', and the movement is compared to European innovators in other fields such as Debussy, Stravinsky, Gauguin, and Matisse. In terms of a literary genealogy the Imagists are described as 'descendants' of the French *Symbolistes*, but distinct in being 'Individualists'. Such claims indicate a change from the conditions under which emerged Pound's 1913 manifestos of Imagism. Situating Imagism within the broader contours of the modern movement in the arts is part of an emerging historiography of modernism in this period. Rather than claiming absolute newness, as the Futurists had done in 1910, *Some Imagist Poets 1916* was aware that, as the third anthology of such verse, it needed to explain how it was located within other cultural formations. Unlike the competitive manoeuvring between competing isms in the pre-war years, Imagism, perhaps due to the climate of conflict during world war, now felt less inclined to dismiss other movements and more willing to take the time to explain their aesthetic position to a broader reading public.

The preface to the 1916 volume is the longest and takes

considerable time exploring the Imagist espousal of a *vers libre* based upon cadence rather than metre. This part of the preface is clearly related to the interests of Lowell and Fletcher in the form known as polyphonic prose, although it does hark back to Pound's 'A Few Don'ts'. In a section on 'Rhyme and Rhythm', Pound argued that it is not necessary that a poem rely upon its music, but if it does it must be good: 'Let the neophyte know assonance and alliteration, rhyme immediate and delayed, simple and polyphonic, as a musician would expect to know harmony and counterpoint and all the minutiae of his craft' (*IP* 132). This suggests that a poet must know the technical side of poetry as well as a trained musician; the idea of a polyphonic rhyme, however, is slightly puzzling, but might be understood in terms of complex rhymes, like near-rhyme or internal rhyming.

The link between music and language, explicitly poetic language, was also one that many writers explored in this period, perhaps prompted by Walter Pater's famous *fin-de-siècle* claim that 'all art aspires to the condition of music'. An interesting example of such interest is Florence Farr, one of W. B. Yeats's London circle and a member of T. E. Hulme's group, the Poets' Club. In 1909 Farr published *The Music of Speech*, which suggested accompanying spoken poetry by a bare sounding of chords on a specially constructed instrument, a psaltery, to emphasize the natural 'melody of words'.[34] Accompanied by Arnold Dolmetsch, Yeats spoke some poems in a 'subtly modulated monotone' in order to demonstrate what Farr called 'song in speech' and that each single word 'has its own significant music'.[35] Farr's ideas were entertained widely and in 1907 she toured North America, visiting New York, Harvard, Chicago, and Boston.

Such experiments might have influenced Pound, who met Farr through Yeats and heard her recitals. Yeats came to believe that Pound's interest in the troubadours, another literary association of music and poetry, was an improvement upon Farr's work: 'it is more definitely music with strongly marked time and yet it is effective speech'. The drawback with Pound, remarked Yeats, was that 'he cannot sing, as he has no voice. It is like something on a very bad phonograph'.[36] Nevertheless, Pound's interest, along with others in this period, perhaps led to his assertion in a 1918 essay that 'Poetry is a composition of words set to music'.[37] Poetry, argues Pound, must be read as if to imaginary music and not as oratory, a possible retort to the 1916 preface, which claims that 'a cadenced poem is written to be read aloud' since poetry is 'a spoken and not a written art'. Lowell, indeed, became famous for her very theatrical recitals of poetry.[38]

Though there is no clear indication that Lowell knew of Farr's work, the invention of polyphonic prose might be understood as yet another experiment in the field of music and language in the early twentieth century. She had certainly read Pound's 'A Few Don'ts', with its reference to polyphonic rhyme, and perhaps more significantly had an active interest in contemporary music.[39] Lucas Carpenter argues that polyphonic prose was named and formulated by Fletcher, even though he gave Lowell the credit for inventing it.[40] This was outlined in Fletcher's article of 1915, 'Miss Lowell's Discovery: Polyphonic Prose'.[41] Most of Fletcher's poems in this form date from 1914–16, but were not published until his 1921 volume, *Breakers and Granite*. Fletcher, like Lowell, credits the French poet Paul Fort for indicating the possibility of polyphonic prose, but saw antecedents in the 'elaborately rhymed prose of Sir Thomas Browne, de Quincey, or Melville, with this addition: that all the wealth of English rhyme, assonance, verbal onomatopoeia, was deliberately woven into it exactly as the masters of polyphony, such as Bach, had woven over their simple chorales the most elaborate contrapuntal forms'.[42] Other possible French antecedents, of whom Lowell and Fletcher were aware, included the prose poetry of Rimbaud and Laforgue.[43]

Lowell's earliest experiments in polyphonic prose echo Fletcher's ideas and also date from 1914. In her volume of that year a number of poems utilized a prose format, including 'The Basket' and 'In a Castle', based upon *vers libre*, or what Lowell preferred to call 'unrhymed cadence' or 'the rhythm of the speaking voice'.[44] In a later article Lowell said that her choice of polyphonic prose was designed 'to find a new form for epic poetry....The modern epic...should be based rather upon drama than upon narrative. This came partly from the greater speed and vividness demanded today of all the arts'.[45] This latter comment shows clearly how Lowell conceived the form to be essentially linked to the modernity of her times, and that to compose a modern epic demanded a modern form, a principle also elaborated in the 1916 preface. Although Lowell called polyphonic prose 'an orchestral effect', she was keen to extend the term beyond its merely musical resonance: it will treat subjects 'at once musically, dramatically, lyrically, and pictorially'.[46] This indicates a sense of polyphony that is closer to the theorist Mikhail Bakhtin's conception of the novel as a polyphonic or many-voiced form.[47] This is certainly borne out in Lowell's own poetry, which frequently extends from the musical basis of polyphony towards a synaesthetic approach that is perhaps most successful when its subject matter is that of the city. Her visits to London in 1913 and 1914 seemed to precipitate her most experimental verse, not only because of her contact with expatriate writers such as Pound and Fletcher, but also because of her sense of the modernity represented by London in this period. *Sword Blades and Poppy Seeds* contains only a few poems, such as 'A London Thoroughfare. 2 A.M.', which take the city 'squalid and sinister' as its subject matter. But it is with her next volume, *Men, Women and Ghosts* (1916), and the Imagist volume of this year, that we see Lowell combine the musical and formalist techniques of polyphonic prose with the many voices of the modernist city. The 1916 anthology has perhaps her most significant exploration of the city using the format of polyphonic prose, the poem, 'Spring Day', discussed in Chapter 5. The comments in the preface on the difference between poetry and prose could only really apply to Lowell, as no other contributor to the volume employed prose poetry and overall Lowell was also the only regular user of prose verse forms.[48]

These early prose statements of Imagist theory deserve, then, to be understood as forms of manifesto, albeit operating at times in a different tenor to that of the more aggressive rhetorics of Futurism or Vorticism. The question of whether Imagist poetry lived up to the laws, rules or principles proclaimed in such documents is an issue considered in the following chapters.

4

Modern Themes

This chapter considers a number of Imagist poems in the light of some of the different theories discussed in the previous chapter. It looks, in particular, at two significant aspects that help delineate the modernism of Imagist verse: the use of a visual concrete language, as theorized by Hulme and Pound; and the employment of images of Orientalism in a variety of the poems. The preface to the 1915 anthology had boldly asserted that 'We believe passionately in the artistic value of modern life', but had qualified this with a dig at the technologically obsessed Futurists: 'there is nothing so uninspiring nor so old-fashioned as an aeroplane of the year 1911' (IP 135). The modern life that Imagism believed in could, to some eyes, look remarkably old-fashioned. However, a closer inspection shows how even poems based upon ancient Greek or early Chinese poetry demonstrate a keen engagement with the modernity of the early twentieth century. Pound, for one, believed that early Japanese and Chinese poetry exhibited precisely the technique of a 'direct treatment of the thing' that he felt was vital for the reform of modern verse in English.

Writing to Harriet Monroe, early in 1915, Pound bombarded the editor of *Poetry* with recommendations upon poetic style. Many of these are familiar from the other Imagist manifestos: poetry must be close to speech; it should eschew 'book words', periphrasis and inversions; the language must be 'simple' and 'hard' with 'no words flying off to nothing'; abstractions are to be avoided, as must clichés and journalese, and the way to escape from these faults is by concentration and 'precision'. One phrase, however, stands out in this letter, exhibiting a stark claim that reveals much about Imagist technique: 'Language is made out of concrete things', writes Pound, adding that it is lazy to use generalizations in 'non-concrete terms' for they are 'the reaction of things on the writer, not a creative act *by* the writer'.[1] Imagist poems, therefore, would be those that exemplified this view of words as concrete things, where the writer acts upon their material, much in the way that a sculptor acts upon a block of stone (an analogy of which Pound was fond). It seems a development of the first principle of 'Imagisme', with the call for a 'direct treatment of the thing' being transferred onto the verbal material of poetry itself. In many ways this statement encapsulates the impact of Imagism upon much later verse in the twentieth century, a tradition that runs from Imagism to Objectivism and the emergence of Concrete Poetry after World War II.

As with many of Pound's theoretical formulations its origin lay elsewhere, and in this case with T. E. Hulme once again. Hulme's lecture upon 'Romanticism and Classicism' (delivered in late 1911 or early 1912) had predicted a sweeping change in the course of poetry in the twentieth century. After a hundred years of Romanticism, Hulme asserted, classical values are ripe for revival. Romanticism, for Hulme, was a kind of hazy belief in the perfectibility of human beings, a 'spilt religion' in which concepts such as heaven and hell are mixed up, a confusion which will 'falsify and blur the clear outlines of human experience' (S 118). Romantic thought lacked Imagistic 'clear edges', and Romantic verse was organized around 'metaphors of flight', again ignoring properly delimited borders. Classical verse, in contrast, displayed a 'dry hardness', and with its profound sense of the finite (S 133) can express clarity and precision, even using the clumsy 'communal thing' of language. In its finite materiality classical verse approximates to the very essence of poetic, as opposed to prose, language. Hulme distinguished poetry and prose in the following fashion:

> In prose as in algebra concrete things are embodied in signs or counters which are moved about according to rules, without being visualized at all in the process. There are in prose certain type situations and arrangements of words, which move as automatically into certain other arrangements as do functions in algebra. One only changes the X's and Y's back into physical things at the end of the process. (S 134)

Prose is rationalized abstraction that, because it lacks visual form, is a language in which 'concrete things' are dematerialized.

Communication in prose is an 'automatic' procedure, conforming to fixed mathematical processes.

For Hulme this kind of abstraction can be countered by poetic language:

> Poetry... may be considered as an effort to avoid this characteristic of prose. It is not a counter language, but a visual concrete one. It is a compromise for a language of intuition which would hand over sensations bodily. It always endeavours to arrest you, and to make you continuously see a physical thing, to prevent you gliding through an abstract process. (S 134)

This theorization of the benefits of a poetic language of concrete visual objects was very influential, since the pleasure of solidity in language was something Pound and other Imagists constantly upheld, seeing it as the way to a more direct poetic discourse. For Hulme solidity took different forms at different times in his work: the early insistence that all 'poetry is an affair of the body' (SW 34) seemed indebted to Bergson's materialism; this was then followed by the claim in 'A Lecture on Modern Poetry' that the new poetry resembles sculpture, more than music, in the way it has to 'mould images... into definite shapes' (SW 66). Certainly this sculptural vision of verse was taken seriously by Imagists such as Pound, and also by, for example, Richard Aldington, who wrote in 1914 that Imagist poems display a 'hardness, as of cut stone'.[2]

The 'visual concrete' language of Imagism can be found in many places. Pound's 'Ts'ai Chi'h', included in *Des Imagistes*, typifies this aspect of the verse:

> The petals fall in the fountain,
>   the orange-coloured rose-leaves,
> Their ochre clings to the stone.
>
> (DI 31)

The poem is based entirely around visual perception of 'things', merely presenting them in a 'direct' fashion without comment by a speaker or by the poet. Indeed, at one level subjectivity is evacuated from this poem since it lacks any pronoun indicating a human subject. If we read a subjective emotion into the poem – imbuing it with loss or regret for example – it is the reader rather than the text in itself that produces this. The falling movement of these petals, minute blobs of visual data, and their clinging attachment to the solidity of the stone replicates Pound's desire to unite words and things. Nothing is abstract here, such as a comment upon the significance of the leaves falling, and there is no attempt to turn the petals into a symbol of anything else, which would detract from the purely physical nature of the image. The most striking feature of the poem is the colourful intensity used to present the leaves, with the bodily sensations Hulme espoused for poetry being reduced merely to a visual pleasure. The poem is purely formal, with the indented second line perhaps indicating the movement of the petals drifting from the rose before they settle on the stone in the final line. But even this motion is, to use Hulme's term, 'arrested' as the poem ends so suddenly: just as the leaves cling to the stone we are left with a poem made of words that cling like things to the page, a poem made out of colourful 'concrete things'.

A similar technique is found in Fletcher's poem, 'The Skaters', included in the 1916 anthology:

Black swallows swooping or gliding
In a flurry of entangled loops and curves;
The skaters skim over the frozen river.
And the grinding click of their skates as they impinge upon the surface,
Is like the brushing together of thin wing-tips of silver.

(SIP 1916 48)

Unlike 'Ts'ai Chi'h' this poem does include human subjects, but yet again focuses upon an objectivity of presentation. We are not really guided into how to view the skaters, we are simply presented with their visual appearance without comment from the author. Although there is some auditory imagery ('the grinding click' of the skates), the dominant style is that of visual and concrete images, tracing patterns in their movements on the ice. The poem employs a recurrent Imagist device, the simile, whereby the skaters are compared to the swallows, but again the basis of the comparison is a purely visual one: the wing-tips of the birds are thus like the silver skates on the ice. Interestingly, the simile is rather ambiguous, for as Gage notes, the opening lines confuse the reader 'by creating an equilibrium between the parts of the comparison...allowing the reader momentarily to view either swallows or skaters in terms of the other'.[3] Though this confusion is clarified by the end of the poem Gage suggests that the effect of untangling the ambiguity is somewhat like the 'entangled loops and curves' of the skaters on the ice. Although the poem contains more dynamism than Pound's 'Ts'ai Chi'h', in terms both of the skaters and birds, and the movement of the simile, the dominant sense of the poem is that of two sets of visual images, arrested and laid out for comparison.

There are, however, other forms of attention to the quidditas of the world to be found in Imagist poetry. H.D.'s 'Oread', which is also structured around a central, but implied simile, offers a more tactile presentation of objects:

> Whirl up, sea –
> Whirl your pointed pines,
> Splash your great pines
> On our rocks,
> Hurl your green over us,
> Cover us with your pools of fir.

(*SIP 1915* 28)

Here the waves of the sea are compared to pine trees, a startling optical comparison in many ways, since the similarity is between the separate realms of sea and land. Although there is much evidence of a concrete visual language, in the references to the shape and colour of the pines, and in the general simplicity of vocabulary and syntax, this is a poem that does not really arrest motion. The use of assonance and alliteration ('whirl', 'hurl', and 'fir'; 'pointed pines' and 'splash') creates a sense of movement through the lines that apes the motion of the sea. More than this, however, the most striking difference from the poems by Pound and Fletcher is the appearance of a subjective dimension: if the other poems presented an objective picture of the objects perceived, 'Oread' offers a 'direct treatment', where the 'thing' is more subjective and part of a more sensual engagement with the world. The poem is an invocation to the sea to 'cover' the nymph of the poem's title. The green of the pines is not placed apart for detached perception, as in Pound's 'orange-coloured rose-leaves', but is an integral part of the thing that touches 'our rocks' and which will 'Cover us'. Echoing Hulme's poetry of the body, this poem does attempt to 'hand over sensations bodily'.

This is not to imply any absolute distinction between those poets who engage in direct treatment of objects and those whose directness is of more subjective matter. H.D.'s poetry, however, is often quite different in its handling of human relations from that of Pound. Take Pound's poem, 'The Encounter':

> All the while they were talking the new morality
> Her eyes explored me.
> And when I arose to go
> Her fingers were like the tissue
> Of a Japanese paper napkin.[4]

In a contemporary essay, 'Vorticism', Pound argued that all 'poetic language is the language of exploration', adding that the Japanese clearly understand this linguistic 'sense of exploration'.[5] Here visual exploration is replaced by the feel of the woman's fingers, recalling the delicacy of Japanese paper. The movement of the text is again away from conceptual abstraction – the morality perhaps referring to Freud's thought – towards the sensuous, the specific and the concrete.[6] It represents Pound's desire to shift from verbal abstractions to the pleasures of 'things', a move that here demonstrates an interesting sexual politics. The exploring hands of the poet defuse the woman's exploring gaze. It is a strategy that reduces her to mere fingers, a synecdoche that then diminishes the woman still further by comparison with the disposable, though possibly sensuous, napkin. Arguably the poet here touches the woman only as a way to stop himself being the object of her gaze. Though the touch of the fingers may in itself be pleasurable, the encounter is much more detached and wary than that experienced in H.D's 'Oread'.

Both of Pound's poems discussed above are linked by their references to 'Oriental' topics. T. S. Eliot claimed in his introduction to Pound's *Selected Poems* in 1928 that 'Pound is the inventor of Chinese poetry for our time'.[7] Though this claim cannot stand sustained examination in today's post-colonial world the nature of Pound's 'invention' or 'exploration' of Chinese and Japanese culture is worth considering as it constitutes an important modern theme within Imagist poetry. In the poem 'Further Instructions' (first published in *Poetry* in

1913), Pound wrote of links he sought to forge between Europe and the Orient:

> I will get you a green coat out of China
> With dragons worked upon it,
> I will get you the scarlet silk trousers
> From the statue of the infant Christ in Santa Maria Novella.[8]

While the latter clothing was quite possibly seen by Pound during his trips to Florence in 1898 and 1908, the dragons he imagines are, not surprisingly, only vaguely located. If Europe was a continent the young Pound had already explored both physically and culturally by 1913, the geography of China was still largely unknown territory, both for Pound and for the other Imagists. The creation of an imaginary geography of the Orient, however, was a very striking feature of Imagist poetry, and one that until recently has received little comment. Conventionally, literary history has indicated how Pound's interest in matters Chinese derived from the influence of figures like Laurence Binyon, or his possession and editing of the manuscripts of the sinologist Ernest Fenollosa as *The Chinese Written Character as a Medium for Poetry*. But a much wider context of influence was that of the visual culture of London in the 1910s and the earlier history of Western interest in 'Japonisme' and 'Chinoiserie'.

One explanation for why Pound and others looked towards the Orient in their poetry can be found in Pound's view of the metropolis as 'that which accepts all gifts and all heights of excellence, usually the excellence which is *tabu* in its own village. The metropolis is always accused by the peasant of "being mad after foreign notions"'.[9] Being 'mad after foreign notions' then, is an urban and modern characteristic for Pound, part of London as a modernist city, where ideas and concepts come rushing in to suffuse the artist with 'newness', helping modernize Western poetry via the 'Orient'. One of the most fascinating forms of 'newness' in London at this time was the imagined geography of the 'Orient' on display in museums, galleries, and exhibitions. How are we to evaluate Pound's cultural encounter with the aestheticized geographies of Japan and China? As modernist exploitation of the 'other', forming part of the multifaceted Orientalist imaginary with which we have become very familiar since the work of Edward Said? Or, as Helen Carr has argued of

Imagist experiments with forms such as the haiku and tanka, is this an example of how Western art did not just absorb Japanese and Chinese cultures, but was 'radically transformed by them. To take the impact of the Japanese haiku less seriously than that of the Italian sonnet is to perpetuate Western disdain for other cultures'.[10] Carr's argument is echoed in the claim by Zhaoming Qian in his book *Orientalism and Modernism* that, 'like French symbolism and Italian culture, Orientalism is a constitutive element of the Modernism of the 1910s and 1920s'.[11]

One significant visual contact zone, for Pound, was the Exhibition of Chinese and Japanese Paintings curated by Laurence Binyon at the British Museum from 1910 to 1912.[12] The exhibition was the largest show in Britain of such work, and contained over 100 Chinese paintings and 120 Japanese works, spanning the fourth to nineteenth centuries. As a result of these, and other, acquisitions the British Museum created an Oriental Sub-Department in 1909. This was the same year that Binyon gave a series of lectures on Oriental art, to which he gave Pound a ticket after their first meeting in February. The lectures were based on Binyon's *Painting in the Far East* (1908), one of the first attempts to produce an appreciation of the aesthetic – rather than archaeological or anthropological – qualities of painting from Japan and China. One painting discussed at length in the book was *The Admonitions of the Instructress to Court Ladies*, which was shown at the 1910 exhibition and which Qian argues inspired Pound to write a number of poems, including the poem 'Fan Piece, for her Imperial Lord' published in *Des Imagistes*:

> O fan of white silk,
>   Clear as frost on the grass-blade,
>   You also are laid aside.

(*DI* 30)[13]

As Qian argues, Pound's poem is a condensation of a number of related influences: the painting exhibited in the exhibition; Binyon's discussion of it; and a poetic account of one of the scenes in the painting, written by its protagonist, Lady Ban, and read in translation by Pound.[14] Pound had found the poem translated in H.A.Giles's influential *A History of Chinese Literature* (1901), which had been given him by Allen Upward. Upward, a lawyer by profession, was extremely interested in Chinese literature and had helped form the Orient Press which published a 'Wisdom of the East' series. In return Pound included some of Upward's prose poems, 'Scented Leaves from a Chinese Jar', in *Des Imagistes*.

Lady Ban was a concubine of the emperor, and the painting depicts her refusing the emperor's invitation to accompany him on a journey. Perhaps as a consequence, a younger woman replaced her in the emperor's affections. Her poem, in Giles's version, expresses her regret at the incident:

> O fair white silk, fresh from the weaver's loom,
> Clear as the frost, bright as the winter snow –
> See! friendship fashions out of thee a fan.

The poem continues to note how the fan, from being a 'close companion' sees itself 'laid neglected on the shelf/ All thought of bygone days, like them bygone'.[15] Pound's version clearly adapts from this poem, but demonstrates the Imagist technique of concision and a focus upon the central simile, comparing the woman to the discarded fan. Pound increases the focus upon a single visual concrete image in the poem in the second line, with the added phrase about the frost on the grass blade. Pound's 'translation' of Lady Ban's poem demonstrates Hulme's call for a period of 'dry, hard classical verse' in which 'beauty may be in small, dry things' (*SW* 78–9). The more extended analysis of Lady Ban's emotions in Giles's version is trimmed back to the essence, whereby the woman is compared to an object, much as we found in Pound's 'An Encounter'. As with a number of poems by Pound and Hulme in this period, the strategy of comparing a female presence to an object suggests a gendering of the terms employed to describe Imagist techniques: a 'dry' verse is seemingly employed to control the perceived 'wetness' of the feminine.

As Qian notes, Pound's poem is close in form to that of a Japanese haiku (with lines of five, seven, and five syllables), a form related to that used in Lady Ban's original.[16] F. S. Flint noted that the pre-Imagist group who first met in Tour Eiffel restaurant in Soho, 1909, with Flint and Hulme among the members, discussed how contemporary poetry might be replaced by 'vers libre, by the Japanese tanka and haiku'.[17] Japanese culture was also much in evidence in London at this time, with a huge Japan-British Exhibition being held in the White City, west London throughout 1910.[18] In a book catalogue from 1910 Elkin Mathews, publisher of Pound's early volumes referred to 'a new Anglo-Japanese Alliance' in literature, referring in particular to the Japanese poet Yone Noguchi, who wrote in English. Pound might have noted an article by Noguchi, published early in 1913 in the magazine *Rhythm*, entitled 'What is a Hokku Poem?'[19] Mathews published a number of Noguchi's books between 1909 and 1914.[20] Noguchi sent a copy of this volume to Pound in 1911, and they corresponded for a number of years.[21] A hokku by Noguchi was later published in *The Egoist* (November 1916), and Pound had written to Noguchi in 1913, suggesting that 'if the east and the west are ever to understand each other that understanding must come slowly and come first through the arts'.[22] Models from Japanese and Chinese culture thus coalesced with European theories about language and style in these poetic experiments.

The 'Orient' provided not only a different poetic form to explore, one committed, like Imagism, to a concision of style, but also in the visual culture of Japan and China a prompt to a poetry rooted in concrete images. Imagism of course drew its influences from a myriad of sources. H.D. and Aldington, for example, modelled many of their Imagist poems upon the verse of ancient Greece, shown in *Des Imagistes* by Aldington's 'To a Greek Marble' and H.D.'s 'Hermes of the Ways'. And though Pound included '△ΩPIA' ('Doria') in the first anthology, he seemed to be very taken with an analogy between Greece and China that he had read about in Binyon's *Painting in the Far East*. Binyon distinguished Chinese from Japanese art arguing that China represents the central tradition of Asian art, since it has, throughout history, had the 'strongest aesthetic instinct'.[23] Japanese art, however, only superficially seems to have improved upon that of China: 'The Japanese look to China as we look to Italy and Greece: for them it is the classic land.... As in the late nineteenth century Japan has taken over the material civilization of Europe, so, more than a thousand years earlier, she took over and absorbed the civilization of China'.[24] This sense of Chinese art as analogous to that of the ancient Greeks certainly caught the attention of Pound, eager to mark out a modern poetry distinct from the forms of English verse in the nineteenth century. In 1914 Pound wrote, with typical hyperbole, that it was 'a time when China has replaced Greece in the intellectual life of so many occidentals'.[25] If Pound had first heard the Greece/China analogy from Binyon's lectures, he also found confirmation in the notes of Ernest Fenollosa, which he edited from the end of 1913 as *The Chinese Written Character as a Medium for Poetry*:

> It is unfortunate that England and America have so long ignored or mistaken the deeper problems of Oriental culture. We have misconceived the Chinese for a materialistic people, for a debased and worn-out race. We have belittled the Japanese as a nation of copyists. We have stupidly assumed that Chinese history affords no glimpse of change in social evolution, no salient epoch of moral and spiritual crisis. We have denied the essential humanity of these peoples.... The duty that faces us is not to batter down their forts or to exploit their markets, but to study and to come to sympathize with their humanity and generous aspirations. Their type of cultivation has been high. Their harvest of recorded experience doubles our own. The Chinese have been idealists, and experimenters in the making of great principles; their history opens a world of lofty aim and achievement, parallel to that of the ancient Mediterranean peoples. We need their best ideals to supplement our own.[26]

Fenollosa's comments here clearly show an attempt of sorts to move past nineteenth-century Orientalism, even if we ponder the nature of the 'supplement' that Japan and China might form in relation to the West.

Lawrence Rainey has characterized Pound's poetic position in 1912 as one of 'living archaism', due to his continued endorsement of the troubadour tradition of Provence, a stance only halted when Pound realized the full implications for the artistic marketplace of Marinetti's explosive impact upon London.[27] His embrace of China might be seen as another mode of archaic thought – certainly the Chinese poets and painters Pound looked to could not be said to represent the future imagined by Marinetti. Perhaps, however, the impact of the Orient on Pound should not simply be conceived temporally, in terms of being either archaic or modern, but spatially, in terms of how the imagined geographies of China and Japan influenced his verse. If Pound learnt how to market modernist verse, specifically the *Des Imagistes* anthology of 1914, from Marinetti, as Rainey claims, it is worth examining whether and how far the use of an imagined geography of the Orient was a branch in that marketing strategy. The anthology contained several examples of Oriental-influenced work: John Cournos's 'The Rose', the sinologist Allen Upward's 'Scented Leaves from a Chinese Jar', and four of Pound's free translations from the Chinese. As Qian shows, Pound was still working on the Imagist anthology at the end of 1913, when he had a series of meetings with Fenollosa's widow, Mary, prior to receiving Fenollosa's papers to edit in December. The confluence of meeting Mary Fenollosa and editing *Des Imagistes* led Pound to write to his future wife Dorothy Shakespeare on 7 October that the Chinese poetry he had been reading was impressive and that 'There is *no* long poem in chinese. The period was 4th cent. B.C. – Chu Yüan, Imagiste'.[28] Perhaps this consolidates Poundian Imagism as archaic – but its antiquity is taken from outside of European models. And for Pound, the influx of non-European images into the contact zone of London produced a different form of dynamism from that celebrated in the technologically obsessed Futurists. In the 'Affirmations' series in the *New Age* of 1915, Pound continued to view China in terms of Greece:

> China is no less stimulating than Greece...these new masses of unexplored arts and facts are pouring into the vortex of London. They cannot help bringing about changes as great as the Renaissance changes...there is life in the fusion. The complete man must have more interest in things which are in seed and dynamic than in things which are dead, dying, static.[29]

Pound's familiar gendered rhetoric of dynamic 'seed' is interesting for the way in which he inverts the stereotypically feminized Orient. Chinese art was thus not regarded as historically outdated, but part of an ongoing geographical and cultural 'fusion' characterizing the metropolitan vortex itself.

Cosmopolitan London was thus a space in which many diverse cultures were represented and it was in this environment that Imagism was forged. In the pre-war years Pound felt that he was 'getting [the] orient from all quarters', visiting restaurants and 'shows chinesesques' (exhibitions) and obtaining 'real japanese prints... at Cedar Lawn [the house of Harriet Shaw Weaver]'.[30] After 1913 Pound was actively interested in Japanese culture, in both his editing of the Fenollosa manuscripts, and an intense collaboration with W. B. Yeats on Noh Theatre, throughout 1915–16. In 1938 Pound wrote of a set of avant-garde Japanese poets who had contacted him: 'All the moss and fuzz that for twenty years we have been trying to scrape off our language – these young men start without it'.[31] Such patterns of transnational modernist influence continued for some time, as is seen in Pound's use of Chinese ideograms in his major work after Imagism, *The Cantos*.

London, with its exhibitions and galleries, thus functioned as a kind of vast contact zone for the geographical display of such countries as Japan and China. A similar line of influence can be noted in two of the American Imagists. In Boston, Amy Lowell and John Gould Fletcher both first encountered the Orient through visual culture. Lowell's elder brother, Percival, lived in Japan for much of her childhood and was responsible for transferring many Japanese works of art to the Boston museum.[32] One of Lowell's most interesting poems taking Japan as its topic is the polyphonic prose poem 'Guns as Keys' (1918). In 1853 the American Commodore Perry had sailed to Japan and demanded that trade be opened up. It is this encounter that forms the subject of Lowell's poem, and in which she says she was opposing 'Oriental craft to Occidental bluff', picturing the 'two races at a moment when they were brought in contact for the first time. Which of them has gained most by this meeting, it would be difficult to say'.[33] Lowell later published the volumes *Pictures of the Floating World* (1919), based on Japanese 'floating world' paintings of the nineteenth century, and collaborated with Florence Ayscough on *Fir-Flower Tablets: Poems from the Chinese* (1921).[34] Lowell's contribution to the 1917 Imagist anthology consisted of a series of poems, 'Laquer Prints', inspired by Japanese haiku.

Fletcher was also influenced by images in a museum display: 'The hours I spent then [1907?] in the Oriental Wing seeing the Sung or Kamakura masterpieces with new eyes, re-educated me in regard to the purposes of a pictorial art close in spirit to my own poetry'.[35] This refers to the Oriental Wing of the Boston Museum of Fine Arts. The pre-eminence of the Boston collection was due to the activities of the turn-of-the-century group known as the 'Boston Orientalists', foremost of whom was Ernest Fenollosa, the first curator of Far Eastern Art in Boston from 1890 to 1896. The impact of the Boston experience led Fletcher to publish the poems *Goblins and Pagodas* (1916) and *Japanese Prints* (1918).

Imagism's belief in the 'artistic value of modern life' thus led the poets in diverse directions for influences and themes. For Pound, and perhaps to a lesser extent Lowell and Fletcher, one important direction was to the visual and verbal culture of Japan and China. To Pound in particular it seemed that the 'visual concrete' language theorized by Hulme for modern poetry could be found not only in the contemporary French poets introduced by Flint, or the austere Hellenicism of H.D., but also in the arresting images of Chinese and Japanese culture. To some critics such use of non-Western cultures is a form of modernist imperialism, whereby the Oriental 'other' is colonized and snatched for Western use. For other critics Imagism's engagement with non-Western forms of representation is part of its endemically cosmopolitan nature. As Helen Carr notes, Imagism was part of a modernist sensibility aware that 'the West was only part of the world's culture'; European modernism was thus opened up and 'radically transformed' by this awareness of other cultural practices. One example, suggests Carr, is that of the modernist practice of collage, a form of writing that enters Anglo-American poetry through the Imagist adoption of the haiku.[36] Such a condensed and visual style of writing was to prove vital when Imagists turned to represent one of the most significant aspects of modernism, that of the city.

5
Urban Images

Some overlook the fact that the most renowned Imagist poem, Pound's 'In a Station of the Metro', is actually a poem about a characteristically urban and modern experience, the mundane fact of travel by underground railway: 'The apparition of these faces in the crowd;/ Petals on a wet, black bough'. One of the dominant ways to read the poem has been influenced by Hugh Kenner's brilliant analysis in *The Pound Era* (1971), where the Paris Metro of the title gives way to a symbolic underworld: 'this is not any crowd, moreover, but a crowd seen underground, as Odysseus and Orpheus and Koré saw crowds in Hades'.[1] Locating Pound's poem within this literary geography, however, loses as much as it gains, since although it allows us to trace another lineage for the classical influences in Pound's verse, or indeed in modernism more generally, it takes the poem away from the material spaces of the modernist city. Pound's poem is about making sense of a particular urban experience, the individual lost but finding beauty amidst the mass of a crowded Metro station. To understand it fully, I would argue, requires us to understand how the early twentieth-century environment found in cities such as London and Paris was registered in the formal structures and styles of Imagist poetry. Pound's Metro *hokku*, an adaptation of an ancient Japanese form, seemed to match the experience of glimpses of faces caught in the new urban spaces of modernism. Since 'In a Station of the Metro' is the most well-discussed of such Imagist poems of the city, this chapter shifts the focus to some of the other poems that treat the urban experience.[2] In particular this chapter examines images of the urban experience by Flint and Fletcher and also Lowell's application of 'polyphonic prose' to the representation of the city.

Interestingly, some other Imagist poems in addition to Pound's 'Metro' took urban transport as their setting. Aldington published 'In the Tube' in *The Egoist* in 1915, two poems by Flint, 'Tube' and 'Accident' are set on trains, and Fletcher published a long poem about commuting across the city, 'London Excursion', in the 1915 anthology. All of these poems present markedly similar scenarios: the poet or protagonist examines fellow passengers, often focusing upon their eyes, and then discerns an antagonist set of relations between these mutual gazes. In Aldington's 'In the Tube' the poet confronts 'A row of eyes,/ Eyes of greed, of pitiful blankness' that he then realizes are staring at his own eyes. This produces a sense of 'Antagonism,/ Disgust,/ Immediate antipathy' which concludes with the poet finding that he shares the same menacing thought as his fellow passengers: 'What right have you to live?'[3] In Flint's 'Tube' the focus is once more negative, and once again upon the gaze of other passengers: 'You look in vain for a sign,/ For a light in their eyes. No!' Flint's 'Accident' (first published in *Poetry*, 1913) offers a rather more positive engagement upon the train and concerns an unfulfilled visual encounter with a stranger:

> Dear One! you sit there
> in the corner of the carriage;
> and you do not know me;
> and your eyes forbid.
>
> (*SIP 1915* 58)

The poet singles out this person, probably female, from the 'wear of human bodies,/ and the dead faces of our neighbours'. Despite the forbidding eyes the poet expresses desire, 'tense and tender', for the unknown passenger, a feeling that is finally thwarted when the poem concludes: 'This is my station...' This poem recalls Pound's 'Metro', which also focuses upon the 'faces' of fellow travellers and seeks to find a transcendent image amidst the anonymous crowd. This is most noticeable in Pound's account of the composition of 'In a Station of the Metro', which attaches special emphasis to his vision of unknown faces: 'Three years ago in Paris I got out of a "metro" train at La Concorde, and saw suddenly a beautiful face, and then another and another, and then a beautiful child's face, and then another beautiful woman'.[4] The stress on the suddenness of the incident accords with the 'sudden liberation' of the Imagist complex that Pound had theorized in 'A Few Don'ts':

> An 'Image' is that which presents an intellectual and emotional complex in an instant of time.... It is the presentation of such a 'complex' instantaneously which gives that sense of sudden liberation; that sense of freedom from time limits and space limits... which we experience in the presence of the greatest works of art. (*IP* 130)

In the Metro poem this sense of the instant is emphasized by the separated set of faces Pound describes; these are particular faces that Pound seems unwilling to combine, the cumulative syntax of 'and then' and 'another', stressing their discreteness. The beauty that Pound seeks inheres not in the crowd or particular people, but merely in their faces.

This recurrent pattern of glances upon faces and eyes of course suited a poetry of images committed, as Hulme had argued, to a visual concrete language. But the occurrence of this visual aesthetic is also tied to the urban environment itself, as the sociologist Georg Simmel had argued in 1903:

> Someone who sees without hearing is much more uneasy than someone who hears without seeing.... Interpersonal relationships in big cities are distinguished by a marked preponderance of the activity of the eye over the activity of the ear. The main reason for this is the public means of transportation. Before the development of buses, railroads, and trams in the nineteenth century, people had never been in a position of having to look at one another for long minutes or even hours without speaking to one another.[5]

For Simmel urban transport altered the pre-existing forms of human relationship, with looking now usurping speaking, intensifying psychic unease in the metropolis. It is hardly surprising, therefore, that Imagist poems reduced fellow passengers to visions of eyes and faces, and that sometimes these faces were figured as threatening presences. Negotiation of city space via new forms of transport such as the tube was an ambivalent phenomenon as the feminist historian Elizabeth Wilson argues: searching for meaning in the city takes various forms, 'not the least important of which is to create new forms of beauty'. However, such beauty 'will never be without a kind of unease', suggests Wilson.[6] One must cope with the anxieties of the new spaces, and their specific visual regimes, but also celebrate the fresh experiences and pleasures offered. Initial reactions to spatial change often consist of mourning the loss of established sureties. But these changes also represent the myriad possibilities of modern metropolitan life, to be transformed and recorded as instances of aesthetic beauty, as the poems by Pound and Flint attempted.

In the Imagist issue of *The Egoist* Aldington had described Flint as 'the poet of modern London' and so it is fitting that in *Des Imagistes* only one poem takes the city as its theme, Flint's 'London'.[7] The only Imagist to be born in London, Flint came from a working-class background that uniquely marked his view of the modernist metropolis. He left school at 13 to take a variety of unskilled jobs, educating himself at night school and developing an interest in European literature and languages. Flint's background entailed a keen interest in the quotidian aspects of life in the modern city, and his extensive reading in contemporary French poetry demonstrated examples of how the city was the perfect topic for a modern, experimental form of writing. 'London' takes up the idea of trying to discover 'beauty' amidst what, for Flint personally, must have been a very harsh material existence:

> London, my beautiful.
> it is not the sunset
> nor the pale green sky
> shimmering through the curtain
> of the silver birch,
> not the quietness;
> it is not the hopping
> of birds
> upon the lawn,
> nor the darkness
> stealing over all things
> that moves me.

(*DI* 31)

This poem's modernity shows how innovative Flint was in comparison to some of the other contributors to *Des Imagistes*. Pound's contributions, aside from the formal experiment of 'The Return', were translations of oriental texts, while Aldington and H.D. offered verse that was heavily indebted to classical Greek models (see, for example, 'Hermes of the Ways', 'To Atthis', or 'Choricos'). Flint's poem, only given the title 'London' later, is startling both for its use of free verse (what he called 'unrhymed cadence') and for the contemporary nature of its subject matter. No other contribution to the volume, for example, forsakes capitalization for the initial word of most lines. Pound would occasionally drop initial capitals, but normally only for heavily indented lines, such as the closing lines of 'The Return':

> Slow on the leash,
>   pallid the leash-men![8]

Flint's approach to capitals, probably picked-up from contemporary French poets, was to become a popular marker of modernist free verse, being particularly associated with H.D. and William Carlos Williams, but it is noticeable that other poems by Flint in *Des Imagistes* are in this form.[9] Effacing the capitals increases the effect of the run-on clauses in the poem, adding to the movement of phrases such as the darkness 'stealing over all things/ that move me'. Arguably, it also adds to the visual quality of the poetry by providing fewer spatial breaks in the typography of the text. Other features of the style, such as the direct syntax, lack of ornamentation and simplified diction, mark this as an excellent example of the Imagist form.

Paradoxically the beauty that Flint ascribes to the city is mainly found in the natural images of the moon and the wind in the final stanzas:

> London, my beautiful,
> I will climb
> into the branches
> to the moonlit tree-tops,
> that my blood may be cooled
> by the wind.
>
>   (*DI* 31)

This strategy is not, however, a rejection of the city for lacking the beauty of natural phenomena, since the epithet 'beautiful' is repeated about London alone. Rather the poem celebrates precisely the presence of the moon in the urban environment and 'the glow her passing/ sheds on men'.

Finding beauty in the modern city is a characteristic of many of Flint's poems, and can be contrasted sharply with two poems in *Some Imagist Poets* (1916) by Aldington that bemoan the problematic status of beauty in the city. 'Eros and Psyche' and 'Whitechapel' both describe specific locations within London but contrast the physical surroundings with Greek signifiers of beauty. 'Eros and Psyche' concerns a 'grimy statue' of these two figures from Greek mythology found in a 'dull yard near Camden Town/ Which echoes with the rattle of cars and 'buses' (*SIP 1916* 3). Aldington cannot understand why this statue is to be found in 'all this clamour and filth' and is not situated in a 'sun-lit room/ Hung with deep purple, painted with gods' (*SIP 1916* 4). Unlike Flint or Pound in his image of sensuous 'petals' amidst the bleak surroundings of the Paris Metro, Aldington can find no redemption for the statue; as he peers at it 'from a 'bustop' he sees

> ...the limbs that a Greek slave cut
> In some old Italian town,
> I see them growing older
> And sadder
> And greyer

(*SIP 1916* 5)

Much the same message is found in 'Whitechapel', where the East End location is reduced to 'Noise, iron, smoke;/ Iron, iron, iron'. The city here is part of a 'nation maddened with labour;/ Interminable collision of energies' which results in a world 'Speechless, impotent'. Tellingly, Aldington's description of the city is contrasted with two italicized stanzas that depict a welcoming natural environment with swallows, kittiwakes, and 'the silence and green/ Of meadows Apriline' (*SIP 1916* 8–9). Beauty here is clearly located away from the city, unlike Flint's image of 'London, my beautiful'.

The Imagist anthologies also contain three interesting poems by Flint that take London during the First World War as their subject matter. 'War-Time', in *Some Imagist Poets 1916*, is again in uncapitalized *vers libre*, and presents two choices for the protagonist once they leave a house. To the left takes the poet into a suburban setting of gardens with privet hedges and 'the almond blossom shaming/ the soot-black boughs'. To the right takes the protagonist into a more dynamic urban setting:

to greater and greater disquiet;
into the swift rattling noise of the motor-busses,
and the dust, the tattered paper –
the detritus of a city –
that swirls in the air behind them.

(*SIP 1916* 63–4)

At first sight it appears that this will present a rather negative cityscape, with the use of terms like 'disquiet' and 'detritus' signifying this view. But the protagonist moves on and now reaches an extremely busy crossroads in the city, where 'five roads/ meet with five tram-routes'; here, amid the din of 'clangorous tram-cars', we learn the reason for the unease: 'the news is shouted,/ and soldiers gather, off-duty'. It is the war that has broken the tranquil beauty of the city in the path not chosen, and Flint finishes with a statement whose rather convoluted syntax matches the disruption to the city he loves:

Here I can feel the heat of Europe's fever;
and I can make,
as each man makes the beauty of the woman he loves,
no spring and no woman's beauty,
while that is burning.

(*SIP 1916* 64)

Though perhaps offending the Imagist dictum of presentation here, Flint's poem suggests that the city itself, and its own individual beauty, is threatened and cannot be 'made' when the fever of war is upon it.

Flint's poems, 'Searchlight' and 'Zeppelins', from the 1917 anthology, admirably capture this sense of an urban experience strained by war:

There has been no sound of guns,
no roar of exploding bombs;
but the darkness has an edge
that grits the nerves of the sleeper.

(*SIP 1917* 55)

The reference to the disturbed 'nerves' here in the poem 'Searchlight' indicates how the war produced civilian war neuroses – such as insomnia – that were distinct from, though related to, the more commonly understood phenomenon of combatant 'shell shock'.[10] The sleeper is puzzled as to why he has woken, since 'nothing disturbs the stillness' of the night. But as he goes to the window it is revealed that his disturbance was caused by the searchlight, 'a beam of light, miles high,/ dividing the night into two before him,/ still, stark and throbbing'. The searchlight is imagined as a threatening phallic object, a 'great beam thrusting back into heaven', beneath which the city seems to cower: 'The houses and gardens beneath/ lie under the snow/ quiet and tinged with purple' (*SIP 1917* 56). Though the poem starts with the reference to the effect upon the sleeper's nerves, the main interest is upon how the city itself is visually altered by the searchlight. The visual concrete language of Imagist theory is here put to excellent use, capturing both the subjective and objective dimensions of the scene.

Zeppelin raids on London began in 1915, with aeroplane attacks in 1917. The idea of war from above was a new and terrifying experience for the inhabitants of London that only added to the 'grit' in the nerves of the population. H.D. produced a brilliant picture of London under attack in the autobiographical novel of her life with Aldington, *Bid Me to Live*, started in the late 1930s but not published until 1960. London here is figured as a city of death: 'Ashes and death; it was a city of dreadful night, it was a dead city'.[11] Flint's poem 'Zeppelins' commences, like 'Searchlight', in the bedroom demonstrating the intrusion of the war into the domestic realm. However, in this poem stillness is replaced by voices and the clamour of warning bells. The protagonist hears explosions and sees the glow of fires, but is unable to catch sight of the zeppelin. He climbs to the top of the building to try to see the attacking dirigible:

> There is nothing to see...
> But the silence and stillness are sinister.
> What has been taken away, what added?
> Brick and stone have become unreal,
> and only the primaeval trees remain,
>   with the primaeval fear behind them and among them....
>
> (*SIP 1917* 59)

Flint's focus is once again upon how the city, rather than its specific inhabitants, is transformed by the attack, with the physical environment being made 'unreal' and with 'fear' seeping into its very fabric. Though this poem is rather longer, and more narrative in style, the directness of the diction and the visual clarity of the images are very much in keeping with Imagist theory. While T. S. Eliot, like Aldington, was to view London as an essentially 'Unreal city', Flint's images of London seem more attentive and personally involved, taking care to indicate the threats that can make the urban experience unreal and fearful, as well as beautiful.

John Gould Fletcher wrote of London as an American exile, first visiting the city in May 1909 and remaining, on and off, until 1920. Fletcher later noted how he found in 'the surging, moving mobs of Oxford St., Piccadilly, the Haymarket, and the Strand a democracy of effort and a spirit' encapsulated in the poetry of Walt Whitman.[12] In 1913 Fletcher financed the publication of five of his own books of poetry, including *The Dominant City*, in which he tried to 'describe the essence of a modern city' in terms more influenced by French poets such as Baudelaire.[13] This influence is clearly noticeable in the subject matter of the poems, covering topics such as walking the streets at night and the prostitute as urban commodity. Another poem, 'The Hoardings', examines the pervasive visual culture of advertisements in the city: 'I see hoardings row on row,/ Flare in pink and yellow dyes./ Glittering promises they bear;/ Food to gorge and drink to swill'. Intriguingly, Fletcher does not dismiss these images:

> Poet do not vainly dream
> Of a past forgot for long,
> Let the wonderful hoardings stream
> In their splendour through your song.
>
> Fling away the beautiful,
> Withered flowers of ancient birth:
> See! It springs in blossom full,
> Fresh from out the teeming earth.[14]

The poem is interesting both for the way it attempts to naturalize the city, with the advertisements springing like flowers from the earth, and for the sense that they symbolize a modernity to which the poet should aspire. However, the form of this poem, and the others in the volume, marks these as non-Imagist, shown in the strict metre and rhyme scheme, the rhetorical diction ('See!') and the clichéd adjectival usage ('vainly dream'). Arguably, the emphasis on images of nature demonstrates a poem unable to fully comprehend the metropolis in a new modernist vocabulary.

A comparison with one of Fletcher's poems, 'The Unquiet Street' from *Some Imagist Poets 1916*, shows how his work developed after meeting Pound and Lowell in 1913:

> By day and night this street is not still;
> Omnibuses with red tail-lamps,
> Taxicabs with shiny eyes,
> Rumble, shunning its ugliness.
> It is corrugated with wheel-ruts,
> It is dented and pockmarked with traffic,
> It has no time for sleep.
> It heaves its old scarred countenance
> Skyward between the buildings
> And never says a word.
> On rainy nights
> It dully gleams
> Like the cold tarnished scales of a snake:
> And over it hang arc-lamps
> Blue-white death-lilies on black stems.
>
> (*SIP 1916* 42)

This is a more defiantly urban poem that resists transformation into nature. Even the final simile, comparing the street to a snake and then lilies, does not retreat from the urban setting as the earlier poem appeared to do. The inability of the street to articulate (it 'never says a word') can be taken as an Imagist refusal to symbolize, merely presenting images like blank paper inscribed by the objects of urban life. The traffic indelibly marks the street, but there is no attempt to generalize these images into any outright claim about the positive or negative value of city life. Indeed, although busy with traffic human subjectivity is seemingly absent in this poem. Instead broken signs of the body are turned into street objects: taxicabs have 'eyes'; the street has a 'pockmarked' and 'scarred' face unable to sleep or speak. Formally, the free verse here employs short, often end-stopped lines, to good effect, emphasizing a set of disjointed fragments in a modernist metropolitan moment.

Another poem by Fletcher in the same anthology, 'The Empty House', continues this urbanization of the human body. The poet leans from his windowsill to view a row of houses opposite, concentrating upon 'the only house that lives/ In all that grim four storied row'. This house is said to possess a 'silent swarthy face' and the personification continues:

> Eyelessly proud,
> It watches, it is master;
> It sees the other houses still incessantly learning
> The lesson it remembers,
> And which it can repeat the last dim syllable of.
>
> (SIP 1916 47)

Here the urban environment is slightly more intimidating, with the protagonist being confronted by a mutant human form; they gaze at each other and the human eye retreats to consider why this house is 'master' of the others. The house seems imbued with some undisclosed meaning, since it knows the 'last dim syllable' that the other houses are still learning. Possibly the 'lesson' is that the physical environment of the house will outlive that of its inhabitants. The puzzle recalls Elizabeth Wilson's re-reading of Freud's theory of the uncanny, stressing its appearance in urban contexts. For Wilson, in the city 'empty streets are sources or sites of the uncanny. It is precisely because there is "nothing there" that fear comes to fill this vacuum'.[15] In Fletcher's poem the lack of human life provokes the fantasy that the house is itself animate and more powerful than any human form.

Fletcher's most sustained engagement with the city is to be found in his series poem 'London Excursion', published in part in *The Egoist* in 1914 and then in full in *Some Imagist Poets 1915*. Harold Monro, writing in the special Imagist issue of *The Egoist*, noted with some regret how Imagist 'minds are obsessed by the Town' and that 'the passing event and its effects on their minds is everything to them'.[16] Referring to Fletcher's 'London Excursion', Monro struggles to like the poem, concluding with the faint praise that 'if the design of art be to represent accurately, this poem, in being as ugly as what it represents, is true to that design'.[17] Fletcher's poem certainly exhibits an ambivalent attitude towards one particular aspect of city life, the journey in and out of the city from the suburbs, but the poem is perhaps more interesting than Monro's comment suggests. As

Bryony Randall argues, the poem pre-dates more well-known images of the city in modernist poetry, such as T. S. Eliot's *The Waste Land*, and 'provides an early example of the now-familiar figure of the alien subject in a mechanized environment, yearning for release from the importunate city'.[18]

The poem is in nine sections, tracing a journey by bus and on foot from 'Great walls of green' to a distant city. Biographically, this journey was one Fletcher took from the Kent suburb of Sydenham into the centre of London to meet the other Imagist poets. The word 'Excursion' is interesting in this connection, since it indicates a journey taken not for work, unlike many of the other figures in the poem, but more for sightseeing, as if on holiday. Fletcher's position as a stranger to this city informs this detached view of London, in a way very distinct from the native visions of Flint. The initial journey on the 'red bulk' of a bus takes the protagonist into 'the angular city' composed of 'Black coarse-squared shapes' (*SIP 1915* 40). Fletcher had visited Paris in 1911 and 1912 and had developed a keen interest in contemporary movements in painting such as Post-Impressionism and Cubism. This awareness seems to inform the depiction of the city in 'London Excursion', with the repeated references to angles and cubes to describe the buildings: 'The city forcing up through the air/ Black cubes close piled and some half-crumbling over'. Against these harsh angles the protagonist revolts: 'I bend, I twist myself,/ I curl into a million convolutions:/ Pink shapes without angle' (*SIP 1915* 41). For Fletcher the human form is not shaped like the city and he desires an escape that is thwarted when the jolt of the bus forces 'a long hot bar' (presumably on the bus seat) into his back, a physical reminder of how the urban environment projects into the psyche of the city-dweller. The poet leaves the bus for a section entitled 'Walk', and now, as the more traditional *flâneur* discerned by Baudelaire, he achieves a degree of independence, 'Insinuating myself into self-baffling movements' as 'Lazily I lounge through labyrinthine corridors'. He then attempts to make sense of the vertiginous urban experience:

> Roses – pavement –
> I will take all this city away with me –
> People – uproar – the pavement jostling and flickering –
> Women with incredible eyelids:

> Dandies in spats:
> Hard-faced throng discussing me – I know them all.
> I will take them away with me,
> I insistently rob them of their essence,
> I must have it all before night,
> To sing amid my green.
>
> (*SIP 1915* 45)

The poet seeks to take these fragmentary images and 'know them', promising himself to capture the 'essence' of urban experience and render it in a poem, recalling Pound's Imagist 'complex' with its sense of freedom and liberation. This active subjectivity is, however, soon lost as he is 'blown like a leaf/ Hither and thither' and eventually decides that 'I can no longer find a place for myself' in the city. As he arrives back, in the section 'Station', into his wall of green, the protagonist finds himself alone and as he looks back he sees 'The city has grown', an image of how the city has somehow defeated his attempt to revolt against it and, arguably, also his attempt to depict the 'essence' of the city in his poem.

Fletcher later reflected upon his method for composing a poetry of the city, a method that tried to describe the objects perceived without in any way identifying with them:

> I would try and put down their essence, their moods, so to speak, by finding words and colour sounds that would orchestrate them, make them speak to the reader by means of such combinations. I would thus try and get at the dominant moods of the city.... Then I would take in other objects... the banks, the hospitals, the churches, the hotels, the clubs, the theatres, the stores, the street traffic, the railway stations, the restaurants, the parks, the public houses, the street corners. Thus the whole city would become re-created in my mind by grasping the objects in it simply as objects and as nothing more. That seems to me to be the essence of what the imagists are trying to do. The trouble with them is that they cultivate too much the fragment. They haven't tackled yet, in perfectly free form, a whole city full of people.[19]

The intention was thus for the poet to register the multiple images of the city, and then to 'orchestrate' the objects perceived without excessive comment or analysis. 'London Excursion' is, I think, only partly successful judged against these criteria, as the protagonist is too clamorous in his mission to capture aesthetically the essence of the metropolis. The use, at times, of an elevated 'poetic' style and diction also slightly undercuts Fletcher's work: 'O angle-builders,/ Vainly have you prolonged your effort', he writes, using just the sort of inversion of natural speech ('Vainly have you') that the Imagist prefaces denounced. Fletcher's criticism that Imagism relied too much upon the 'fragment' and that the diverse mass of the city demanded a different poetic technique in order to capture its myriad features is worth consideration. Partly it indicates Fletcher's own ambivalence about being labelled an Imagist. And to an extent it relates to a point made by Pound about the inherent problem of writing a long Imagist poem. But Fletcher's method of attempting to 'orchestrate' the fragmentary images and moods of the city into a larger work points to another innovation in free verse to be found in both his work, and that of Amy Lowell, the poetry they called 'polyphonic prose'. In 'London Excursion' Fletcher referred to how 'The city about me/ Resolves itself into the sound of many voices', and the experiments of polyphonic prose by certain Imagists attempted to represent the plurality of these urban voices.

Some Imagist Poets 1915 was the first anthology to highlight polyphonic prose, with Lowell's war poem 'Bombardment' closing the volume. Earlier that year Fletcher had written an article on 'Miss Lowell's Discovery: Polyphonic Prose', for *Poetry* magazine. The 1916 Imagist anthology, the second to be produced under Lowell's stewardship, has perhaps her most significant exploration of the city using the format of polyphonic prose, the poem 'Spring Day'.

'Spring Day' enacts a sensual engagement with the hubbub of the city, before withdrawing to regard it from afar through the use of tropes of nature.[20] The city is not, however, negatively portrayed in comparison with the flowery garden, as the poet is 'proud' to feel the pavement and is said to be 'part' of the city, merged into its fibres. Like Fletcher's 'London Excursion', 'Spring Day' is a series poem, composed of five sections, and follows the protagonist from an early morning bath to sleep at night-time in a single day. This exploration of the day, and dailiness in all its mundanity, is also of interest, as it is prior to Joyce's setting of his novel *Ulysses* on a single summer's day. Though Lowell's poem is conceived on a much smaller scale than Joyce's work, it contains something of the same sense of the ordinary and quotidian as significant topics for modernism. And, like Joyce, something of the heroic capacity to endure and flourish in the condition of modernity is also evident in this poem. In order to capture the sense of newness represented by modernity what better place to start than with the sensation of the everyday, rather than with the extraordinary?

Nothing remarkable happens in Lowell's poem, merely breakfast and a walk through the city, but the poem's attempt to transform routine into an instance of beauty is characteristically Imagist and modernist. One of the devices Lowell uses to produce this is her focus upon synaesthesia, with the 'smell of tulips and narcissus in the air' a phrase that is repeated throughout the poem. The opening section describing the bath focuses upon the visual play of light upon water, as the sunshine pours through the window and 'cleaves the water into flaws like a jewel, and cracks it to bright light' (*SIP 1916* 82). The protagonist lies back in the bath and lets the 'green-white water, the sun-flawed beryl water, flow over me', the sensuous qualities of the light and water being repeatedly stressed.

Much the most successful section of 'Spring Day' is the section 'Midday and Afternoon', which is set amid the bustling streets of the city. This is because the formal polyphonic devices Lowell utilizes find a more appropriate content in the phenomenology of the modern city:

> Swirl of crowded streets. Shock and recoil of traffic. The stock-still brick façade of an old church, against which the waves of people lurch and withdraw. Flare of sunshine down side-streets. Eddies of light in the windows of chemists' shops, with their blue, gold, purple jars, darting colours far into the crowd. Loud bangs and tremors, murmurings out of high windows, whirling of machine belts, blurring of horses and motors. A quick spin and shudder of brakes on an electric car, and the jar of a church bell knocking against the metal blue of the sky. I am a piece of the town, a bit of blown dust, thrust along with the crowd. Proud to feel the pavement under me, reeling with feet. Feet tripping, skipping, lagging, dragging, plodding doggedly, or springing up and advancing on firm elastic insteps. (*SIP 1916* 84–5)

Here the poetic effects of rhyme, assonance, alliteration, and return enhance the claims of polyphonic prose to be orchestral and many-voiced, as Lowell creates a kaleidoscopic urban panorama. The irregular rhymes of the opening lines (Shock/ stock; traffic/ brick; church/ lurch) add to what Lowell terms the 'tonal colour'[21] of the aural picture of the city. Arguably, a regular rhyme scheme cannot represent the haphazard sounds, the 'loud bangs and tremors' that one encounters when walking the streets of the city. This attempt to directly capture the texture of the city derives from the Imagist dictum that *presentation* rather than *representation* was to be the aim of their poetry.[22] Lowell's argument that polyphonic prose is 'an orchestral form' that employs a contrapuntal logic rather than a single melodic line seems ideally suited to the urban soundscape she describes here. One might recall T. S. Eliot's claim in 1921 that the music of Stravinsky's *The Rite of Spring* reminded him of 'the scream of the motor-horn, the rattle of machinery, the grind of wheels, the beating of iron and steel, the roar of the underground railway, and the other barbaric noises of modern life'.[23] Lowell's 'Spring Day' might be read with an ear for the noises of modern life, albeit with the difference that barbarism is tempered with a certain pleasure in the sounds of the city.

In addition to the clatter of the city, Lowell's poem also uses the irregular sentence lengths of polyphonic prose to capture another key aspect of urban life, the effect of movement. Freed from the constraints of the metrical line, we see how the switching between long and short sentences apes the crabby progress of the traffic and pedestrians in the city, shifting forward only to stop and 'recoil' a moment later. Even in the childlike rhyming of the line 'Feet tripping, skipping, lagging, dragging, plodding doggedly' it is the physical patterns of movement in the modern city that Lowell is trying to present. Pound would undoubtedly have derided this sort of verse, perhaps recalling his criticism of Futurism as 'accelerated impressionism'.[24] However, Pound's obsession with an Imagism of hard, clear lines (particularly in his Vorticist phase) can be contrasted with Lowell's form of Imagist attention to the flux and blurred outlines of the city. While Pound's rhetoric of poetic objectivity was designed to master and control the energy of the city, Lowell's poem shows a protagonist happy to drift through the town, like 'a bit of blown dust, thrust along with the crowd'.

Lowell's corporal engagement with the city, emphasizing the contact of feet upon the pavements, does not try to bemoan or contain the urban as Aldington or Fletcher might, but quietly celebrates its powerful qualities. Again, unlike the visual thrust of Poundian Imagism, Lowell's representation of the city equally, and perhaps more so, emphasizes sound and touch.

The final section of the poem 'Night and Sleep' does, however, contain a predominantly visualized city, as Lowell describes the electric advertising signs that 'gleam out along the shop fronts', such as an effervescent mug of beer. Again, however, Lowell tries to employ aural effects to describe these visual images. Some signs 'grow, and grow, and blow into patterns of fire-flowers, as the sky fades', while of another Lowell writes: 'Twinkle, jab, snap, that means a new play; and over the way: plop, drop, quiver is the sidelong sliver of a watchmaker's sign' (*SIP 1916* 84). Raymond Williams once noted that many of the linguistic experiments of the modernist avant-garde could be traced back to certain kinds of 'strangeness and distance' to be found in the metropolis that stemmed from 'the inescapable new uses in newspapers and advertising' of even one's native language. Lowell's images of neon advertisements bear out Williams's claim that the metropolis itself not only stimulated such experiments as polyphonic prose, but also was 'an intense and visually and linguistically exciting process in its own right'.[25]

After this visual bombardment the protagonist retreats to the edge of the city, to where 'the earth of my garden smells of tulips and narcissus'. The repetition of this phrase, an example of what Lowell calls 'return' in polyphonic prose, is interesting since it indicates that the garden is not a pastoral retreat from the sensations of the city. In fact there are 'no flowers in bloom yet' in the garden, and the most pungent smells of tulips and narcissus have occurred in the city when, for example, the poet sees a boy on the street selling newspapers: 'I smell them clean and new from the press. They are fresh like the air, and pungent as tulips and narcissus'. Curiously, then, the odours generated in the city are more real than the smell of actual flowers. This confusion of city and nature continues as the poet looks out of her window: 'I can see the distant city, a band of twinkling gems, little flower heads with no stems. I cannot see the beer glass, nor the letters of the restaurants and shops I passed, now the signs blur and all together make the city, glowing on a night of fine weather, like a garden stirring and blowing for the Spring' (*SIP 1916* 86). City and garden are not contrasted, but seemingly merged, with the flowery smells of the city replacing those of the garden, and the lights of the city being transformed into 'twinkling' flower heads.

Lowell had written, in the preface to her volume *Men, Women and Ghosts* (1916), of how walking in the city was an experience informing poems like 'Spring Day' and 'Towns in Colour': 'It is an enchanting thing to wander through a city looking for its unrelated beauty, the beauty by which it captivates the sensuous sense of seeing'.[26] The idea of 'sensuous seeing' is an intriguing one, and perhaps suggests that other senses are somehow subsumed in the visual or that visuality must somehow be expanded to be more haptic. Certainly, the use of sound and smell in 'Spring Day' supports a more tactile understanding of Imagist 'seeing' than even Lowell imagined in her claim that she was employing a 'purely pictorial effect'.[27] This expanded sense of sight might also help understand the concept of 'unrelated beauty'. 'Unrelated' seems a link to the many voices of the polyphonic prose, a poetry of unrelated rhythmical and tonal effects, where the devices are not joined together by some overarching rhyme or metre but connect or interact in a seemingly random fashion. The prose mimics the beauty of the city, where images are constantly juxtaposed in an accidental fashion to the eyes of the passerby, and where people in the street mingle and meet in chance, unrelated encounters.

In the preface to *Men, Women and Ghosts*, Lowell credited the 'unrelated' method to Fletcher's poem 'London Excursion', with its portrayal of a journey into and out of the city on a single day. Bryher, however, in her appreciation of Lowell's poetry, published in 1918, suggested that Fletcher's poem is dominated by the poet's personality, while Lowell's poem is 'charged... with suggested personality' and has thus 'snared the fluttering day itself'.[28] Bryher's sensitive and enthusiastic account of Lowell's poetry makes much of how Lowell's 'revolution' in verse is able to capture, in a semi-psychoanalytic sense, aspects of modernity hitherto missing in contemporary writers:

> For years I have grieved that poetry was inarticulate of the transient aspects of an hour, some effect of colour, some movement of wind or rain, actually forming an unconscious part of dream, yet apparently unrelated in any way to thought.[29]

In some ways this comment resembles Virginia Woolf's later comments in 'Modern Fiction' upon how contemporary novelists must try to capture the transient inner life of 'the dark places of psychology'.[30] Just as Woolf praised Joyce for avoiding the external materialism of Edwardian realist fiction, so Bryher praises 'Spring Day' for 'its escape from a mere photograph of actuality, in the union of colour with sound and the feeling of Spring, vivid with an intense, though merely suggested individuality... fluid with light'.[31] Bryher links these transient non-photographic images with the nature of the city as a subject matter in the poems 'Spring Day' and 'Towns in Colour':

> It has ever been a delight to wander about a city, noting the traffic, the noise, the street, that owns but three or four unalterable moods, yet daily makes them other with new delicacy of light, but none before Miss Lowell (...) have captured this sense I had unwillingly deemed too mutable, too fluid to be confined by any words.[32]

Perhaps the most illuminating aspect of Bryher's analysis is this stress upon the fluidity of Lowell's verse, a feature I have been arguing stems from the freedom of the many voices of polyphonic prose, and perhaps also from her gendered insights into *flânerie* in the city.[33]

'Towns in Colours' represents a fuller version of the Imagistic city articulated in 'Spring Day'. This is a poem in five sections, each taking a facet of the cities of Boston and New York to present in a semi-objective fashion, without the presence of an observing protagonist as was found in 'Spring Day'. 'Towns in Colour' is thus a kind of anti-*flâneur* poem, with only the briefest of appearances of a protagonist in the poem. Lowell's urban focus is an eclectic one: a shop window in 'Red Slippers', a dining room in 'Thompson's Lunch Room – Grand Central Station', 'An Opera House', rain in State Street and 'An Aquarium'. The emphasis upon colour in the poems certainly suggests that these are, as Lowell claimed, poems devoted to a 'purely pictorial effect, and with little or no reference to any other aspect of the places described'.[34] I will concentrate upon the first poem, 'Red Slippers', as it is the only 'Towns in Colour' to employ polyphonic prose. Even here, however, the pure pictorialism Lowell evinced is broadened by the multiple voices of polyphonic prose. The poem revolves around a sharp visual contrast, between the red slippers on display in a shop window and both the 'grey, windy sleet' of the city streets and the 'white, monotonous block of shops' nearby. The vivacity of the slippers is emphasized by the manifold terms used to describe them: they are variously red, blood, claret, salmon, maroon, crimson, scarlet, vermilion and rose. The slippers stand out as objects of visual pleasure and stimulation amidst the monotonous whites, blacks and greys of the surrounding environment. They are said to 'flood (...) the eyes of passers-by with dripping colour', with their visuality intruding in reflections upon cabs and trams, umbrellas and other shop windows. The poem concludes with Lowell contrasting the slippers with a peculiar display in another shop window of a 'big lotus bud of cardboard' whose petals mechanically open to reveal a 'wax doll, with staring bead eyes and flaxen hair'. Pedestrians are said to ignore the slippers, for 'One has often seen shoes, but whoever saw a cardboard lotus bud before?' This contrast between the artificiality of the flower-doll and the red slippers suggests a form of resistance to the visual commodification of the window display; the poem rejects the more elaborate window display in favour of the merely mundane image of slippers. Lowell's poem can be read as an attempt to transform the everyday object perceived in the window into an instance redolent of aesthetic pleasure and replete with a colourful intensity that stands out against the grey metropolitan surroundings. The poem thus recalls Fredric Jameson's reading of modernism, where the visual pleasure one takes in colourful and sensual images such as those of abstract modernist paintings are designed to 'restore at least a symbolic experience of libidinal gratification to a world drained of it'.[35] That is, an urban world of commodified objects displayed in shop windows.

As well as visual pleasure, however, the slippers also demonstrate the synaesthetic qualities of polyphonic prose. The slippers 'plunge the clangour of billions of vermilion trumpets into the crowd outside, and echo in faint rose over the pavement'; they also 'snap' like 'cracker-sparks of scarlet', and are said to scream their colour into the street. These verbal qualities are matched in Lowell's familiar deployment of alliteration and assonance as poetic effects. This is brilliantly shown in a line such as 'red slippers, myriadly multiplied in the mirror side of the window', where the aural echoing of the words captures the way in which the images of the slippers duplicate in the mirrored windows. There is a kind of euphoria in this poem, with the Imagist drive to present a concrete object spilling over into a more active and 'sensuous sense of seeing'. As part of another resistance to the greyness of the streets or the shop-window commodity, the poem is full of motion, with the slippers described by means of very many active verbs: 'flooding' the eyes of pedestrians, 'jamming' their reflections into passing cars, these very busy slippers also 'plunge', 'spout', and 'swing' forth from their position in the shop window.

The vivacious life of this mundane object is never quite captured in the other poems in the 'Towns in Colour' sequence. 'Afternoon Rain in State Street', written in free verse, is an interesting attempt to describe a street in Boston (Lowell's home city) as if it were a kind of Cubist painting, and recalls Fletcher's similar approach in 'London Excursion': for example, lights in the windows of buildings are imagined as 'Hard cubes of lemon'. Lowell works hard to capture the visual appearance of a machine-like modern city:

> The city is rigid with straight line and angles,
> A chequered table of blacks and greys.
> Oblong blocks of flatness
> Crawl by with low-geared engines,
> And pass to short upright squares
> Shrinking with distance.[36]

But the 'many voices' of the city are seemingly lost here, as the lyric voice of the poet predominates over the polyphonic qualities of the pictured scene. For example, the Custom House Tower, an early skyscraper in the city, is described as a 'four-sided wedge' with a 'perpendicular grey surface', and is depicted purely in terms of its visual qualities with 'cross-hatchings of rain..scratching lines of black wire across it'.

Imagism, then, often sought to depict the modern city in experimental styles of writing, striving to render the multiple voices of the city in almost as many forms of poem, from the two-line epic of Pound's 'In a Station of the Metro' to the series poems of Fletcher and Lowell. Not all Imagist poets saw the city in the same way, and some hardly addressed it at all. Though H.D.'s work, for example, responded to the contemporary world around, she wrote only one poem, 'Cities', that might be said to take urban life as its subject matter, but even then fairly obliquely. The Imagist movement was, however, formed in London, constructed in the networks of cafés, bookshops, and literary groupings that were so prevalent in the modern cities of this period. It is hardly surprising then that many of the Imagists sought to reflect upon the nature of the environment that brought them all together as a cultural formation. The modern metropolis, as many have noted, from Simmel onwards, is a phenomenon in which the visual image dominates over the other senses: Imagism was thus created, and partly defined, by its engagement with the visuality of the city.

6
Gender and Sexuality: 'Amygism' and 'H.D. Imagiste'

A fuller understanding of Imagism as a cultural formation requires attention to how the individual identities of the poets were formed and altered in the group identity of 'Imagism'. The two female Imagists, Amy Lowell and H.D., were distinct from the other poets, in terms not only of their gender, but also that of their sexuality. Though H.D. married Aldington in 1913, she had already experienced an intense attachment to a female teacher, Frances Gregg, while still living in America. In 1918 H.D. met Bryher (Annie Winifred Ellerman), who was to become her lifelong companion, although H.D. also had later relationships with men. Amy Lowell first met the actress Ada Russell in 1912 and in 1914 Russell moved into Lowell's home at Sevenels, near Boston, remaining with her until Lowell's early death in 1925. The work of both women is marked by these various attachments and sexualities, with H.D.'s poems often exploring boundaries and borders, and much of Lowell's poetry exhibiting coded, and not so coded, forms of lesbian desire.

It is only relatively recently that these issues of gender and sexuality have been seen to significantly alter our understanding of Imagism as a movement.[1] Reading gender and sexuality into the Imagist formation also sheds new light on the internal dispute between Pound and Lowell. Pound's dislike of Lowell's version of Imagism (what he termed 'Amygism') cannot therefore be merely viewed as an aesthetic disagreement. For example, Pound's criticism of Lowell, is deeply gendered in its terminology: 'Amygism', Pound wrote, displayed 'sloppiness, lack of cohesion, lack of organic centre in individual poems, rhetoric'; H.D.'s verse, he suggested in 1917, also suffered from a lack of solidity due to the 'flow-contamination of Amy and Fletcher'.[2] Many aspects of Imagist theory, with its vocabulary of 'concrete things', 'objectivity' and 'precision', is thus implicitly gendered, associating poetry with a masculine perception of the craft of verse. However, if Pound viewed Lowell's version of Imagism as lacking these qualities, it cannot simply be attributed to his misogyny or homophobia, evident as these are in many places in his work. For one must remember that the 'hard light, clear edges' of Imagism was first used by Pound to describe the work of H.D. As Cyrena Pondrom has argued, the early poems of H.D. were the 'models' which 'enabled the precepts of imagism to be defined'.[3]

What Pound saw in H.D.'s early verse confirmed some of the ideas about poetry as a 'visual concrete' language that he had heard from T. E. Hulme. For Hulme the vagaries of prose can be countered by poetic language that 'always endeavours to arrest you, and to make you continuously see a physical thing, to prevent you gliding through an abstract process' (S 134). However, Hulme's example of a visual concrete aesthetic demonstrates the gender implications of this aesthetic:

> If you are walking behind a woman in the street, you notice the curious way in which the skirt rebounds from her heels. If that peculiar kind of motion becomes of such interest to you that you will search about until you can get the exact epithet which hits it off, there you have a properly aesthetic emotion. But it is the zest with which you look at the thing which decides you to make the effort. (S 136)

For Hulme poetic language is a compromise for a more physical language of the body, one rooted in the act of looking. The gender politics of this example is of course the problematic issue here, with the sexualized gaze – the 'zest' of looking – determining the appropriate aesthetic emotion. This is clearly a gendered language of the body, deriving from an active male look that arrests female movement. This is shown in numerous places in Hulme's work, such as in the essay 'Notes on Language and Style', when he refers to words as physical things: 'Want to make them stand up...e.g. walking on dark boulevard. Girl hidden in trees passes on other side. How to get this' (SW 46).[4] This slightly sinister example requires what we might call a language of tumescence, such as Hulme argues for earlier in the essay: 'A man cannot write without seeing at the same time a visual signification before his eyes. It is this image which precedes the writing and makes it firm' (SW 39). 'Solidity', he sums up, 'is a pleasure' (SW 39). Hulme's criterion for successful poetry in the key essay, 'Romanticism and Classicism', is also based upon a conflation of visuality, desire, and solidity: 'Is there any zest in it? Did the poet have an actually realised visual object before him in which he delighted?' (S 137).[5] The point here is not simply to invalidate Hulme's theories by reference to his less than progressive gender politics, but rather to illustrate some of the gendered assumptions behind these aspects of Imagist theory.[6]

They were assumptions also found in Hulme's own verse, such as the short poem: 'Her skirt lifted as a dark mist/ From the columns of amethyst'. Here the woman is reduced to her clothing and the solid columns of her legs. In a similar vein Aldington argued that to write a poem about a beautiful woman would involve turning the woman into an 'image'; the resultant poem would possess 'hardness, as of cut stone. No slop, no sentimentality' and could be compared to 'nicely-carved marble'.[7] The implications of these ideas are that women are objects to be gazed at and it is this zestful image which is turned into a detached and static Imagist poem.

The strategies employed by Lowell and H.D. point to a rather different Imagist aesthetic from that theorized by Hulme as a 'visual concrete' language. In their texts the idea that a modern poetry must represent the visual in a 'solid' manner is problematized. In his letter to Lowell complaining about her proposed anthology of Imagism, Pound says, 'I should like the name "Imagisme" to retain some sort of a meaning. It stands, or I should like it to stand for hard light, clear edges'.[8] It is illuminating to consider this aesthetic in connection with the primal scene, to use Freud's idea, of the founding of Imagism when, in the British Museum teashop, Hilda Doolittle showed Pound a poem for which he suggested the title 'Hermes of the Ways'. As Pound 'scrawled' 'H.D. Imagiste' under the poem, he both named the incipient movement he had been contemplating, and recreated Hilda Doolittle as the poet H.D.[9] Though H.D. accepted her renaming, she did resist, initially at least, integration into Pound's movement. When Pound submitted the poems to *Poetry* magazine H.D. wrote to the editor Harriet Monroe requesting that 'when you publish them will you be so good as to sign them "H.D." simply, cutting out the affectation of the "Imagiste"'.[10]

'Hermes of the Ways' might well display a 'hard light' but, as with much of H.D.'s verse, the idea of 'clear edges' is complicated in a poem celebrating the Greek god of boundaries, Hermes, a figure who is found to be 'Dubious/ Facing three ways'. Even the opening image of the poem creates ambiguity:

> The hard sand breaks,
> And the grains of it
> Are clear as wine.

Here the typical Imagist device of the simile is complicated by the way in which the solidity of the grains of 'hard sand' is dissolved into the liquid image of the wine. Pondrom's argument that Pound's Imagist aesthetic of 'hard light, clear edges' was greatly influenced by his reading of H.D.'s poem is perhaps supported by the use of the words 'hard' and 'clear' in the opening lines of the poem. However, the meaning of these lines points towards a movement of dissolution, with the firmness of the sand being broken down by the wind whipping across the shore in the next stanza:

> The wind,
> Playing on the wide shore,
> Piles little ridges,
> And the great waves
> Break over it.

(*DI* 21)

The sand broken into grains like wine is thus echoed by another fluid trope, the waves of the sea. In a sense there is a merging together of three images here: the force of the wind, the waves of the sea, and the grains of sand. All are in motion, with the 'clear edges' between them dissolved. We then meet Hermes, 'Of the triple path-ways', the mythical representative of this state of flux.

The sense of movement in H.D's poem is even more evident when we compare it to another version of the source poem. 'Hermes of the Ways' was originally written by Anyte of Tegea, a Greek female poet from the third century BC. Aldington published a prose version of the same poem in 1915:

> I, Hermes, stand here at the cross-roads by the wind-beaten orchard, near the hoary-grey coast;
> And I keep a resting-place for weary men. And the cool stainless spring gushes out.[11]

In this version the boundaries between land and sea are more clearly delineated, and there is little attention to the motion of the wind across the sea. A further interesting alteration is that Aldington's poem is in the first person, while the protagonist of H.D.'s poem is distinct from the Greek god: 'I know him/ Of the triple path-ways,/ Hermes,/ Who awaiteth'. H.D's poem therefore explores a relationship between two subjects, but one that is very different from that proposed by Hulme or Aldington in their zestful and solid images. H.D's poem emphasizes a boundary between people that might be merged, just as the poem concludes with a final fusing of land and sea: 'Where seagrass tangles with/ Shore grass'.

As a number of critics have noted, much of H.D.'s work is structured around such notions of boundaries, borderlines or liminality.[12] This is also evident in H.D.'s 'The Pool', discussed early in chapter 3, and which also dissents from the prevalent visuality of other Imagist poems:

> Are you alive?
> I touch you.
> You quiver like a sea-fish.
> I cover you with my net.
> What are you – banded one?
>
> (*SIP 1915* 21)

'The Pool' typifies an equivocation between different states, with H.D. querying how the subject can form a relationship with some object. The poet asks of the pool viewed, 'What are you', employing the direct discourse prescribed by Imagist theory, and rooted in a clear perception of an object. The poem, however, figures the relation to the object in terms of touch rather than detached visual pleasure. The poet eschews presenting an image for the representation of an experience of touching: 'Are you alive?/ I touch you'. In jettisoning sight for palpable contact, H.D. attempts, in her direct use of pronouns, to enter into a relationship with the object rather than gaze at it from afar. The pool responds, quivering at the subject's touch, prompting the possibility of a reciprocal relationship that looking, in its aloof Imagist mode, cannot reproduce.

It would be wrong to suggest the poem provides a perfect example of mutually reciprocating relationships, since it ends in uncertainty: 'What are you – banded one?' For a poem concerned with forming relationships between subject and object, and between subject and subject or self and other, the isolation of each line, sharply curtailed and end-stopped, suggests lack of connection. Each line of the poem reads as a discrete perception unable to finally resolve itself into a more unified statement of the pool's identity or nature. The 'banded' pool thus matches the bands or lines of the poem itself, radically divided internally as much as is the external object perceived. Pinning down the nature of the object cognized is futile, as suggested by the image of trying to cover water with a net.

One can read this poem biographically, referring to H.D's bisexual identity, her marriage to Aldington, and her future long-term relationship with Bryher. H.D's sexuality throughout her life remained as fluid and unbounded, we might say, as the lines of 'The Pool', refusing to resolve itself into clarity and definiteness. Pondrom usefully argues that H.D.'s poetry at this time reflects a variety of choices she faced: between Ezra Pound and Frances Gregg; between her American roots and her European experiences after 1911; between the role of muse to Pound or a poet in her own right; and between heterosexual or homosexual desire.[13] In this way her interest in boundaries, and exploring liminal states, refers both to her poetic practice and to her identity as a woman. It also refers, self-reflexively, to her initial unease at being included within the clear-edged borders of Pound's 'Imagiste' movement.

Given this, it is not surprising that so many of H.D's poems, like Hermes, face different ways, and often consist of a complex interaction between an unnamed 'I' and 'You', as in 'The Pool'. A poem like 'The Garden' concerns just such a relationship, with the protagonist trying to grasp hold of a rose:

> You are clear,
> O rose, cut in rock,
> hard as the descent of hail.

> I could scrape the colour
> from the petal,
> like spilt dye from a rock.
>
> (*SIP 1915* 22)

The language of the poem is an exemplary form of Imagism: there are few adjectives, it is direct and concrete in its treatment, and displays an objectivity of presentation. Interestingly, though Pound or Hulme might describe this language as visual and concrete, the experience the poem seeks to depict is a sensuous and not detached one, shifting from the visual image of the 'clear' rose into the attempt to 'scrape' the colour from the image. The first part concludes with another physical image of contact between the I and the you:

> If I could stir
> I could break a tree,
> I could break you.

Of course, as in 'The Pool', it is difficult to discern exactly the nature of the relationship being formed here, but there is an intensity and tactile quality that moves beyond the idea of merely depicting a physical thing. Crucially, this is not a poem portraying 'nicely carved marble', as Aldington put it, but is a rather more desperate attempt to 'scrape' and 'break', to touch and not just stare at a particular object.[14]

There is indeed an anguished quality to much of H.D.'s verse at this time, clearly linked to her difficult personal life throughout 1915–16.[15] In 'Temple – The Cliff' the protagonist exhibits a desperate desire to touch a divine love-object who is out of reach:

> I said:
> Forever and forever must I follow you
> Through the stones?
> I catch at you – you lurch.
> You are quicker than my hand-grasp.
>
> (*SIP 1916* 27)[16]

Unable to grasp the god on the cliff edge, the protagonist feels 'splintered and torn' and contemplates hurling herself off the rock to reach the temple. This sense of despair is continued in H.D's next contribution to this anthology, 'Mid-day', where the lyric I is imagined as a 'split leaf' that is 'anguished – defeated'. Even though this poem might be said to offend against Imagist objectivity in its presentation of a tormented emotional state, the emotions are still depicted by means of highly concretized images and a typically Imagistic use of simile: 'A slight wind shakes the seed-pods./ My thoughts are spent/ As the black seeds/.../ I am scattered like/ The hot shrivelled seeds' (*SIP 1916* 30). In poems like these it is tempting to see the divisions between I and you not merely as symbolizing relations between H.D. and other people, but as also depicting an inner struggle within her own sense of self, as both a person and a poet. In 'Pygmalion', in *Some Imagist Poets 1917*, the poem explores the nature of creativity and the poet asks directly:

> Which am I,
> The stone or the power
> that lifts the rock from the earth?
> Am I the master of this fire,
> is this fire my own strength?
>
> (*SIP 1917* 25–6)

The use of questioning indicates the uncertainty H.D. still felt about her work, even after several years of being a poet, developing from 'stone' or muse to Pound and Aldington, to an animating 'power' of creativity itself. Again, the borders between different states (a physical object or the power that lifts it from the earth) is the place where H.D.'s poetry continues to reside, resisting some of the 'clear edges' of Pound's Imagism, but exemplifying much else that defined the Imagist movement.

The tactile quality and revision of Imagist 'visuality' that can be discerned in H.D's work can also be noted in much of Amy Lowell's verse. In a number of her texts eyes and looking are oppressive, prying features. In 'Sultry', flowers and fruits become evil eyes assaulting the poet: 'Leopard eyes of marigolds crouching above red earth,/ Bulging eyes of fruit and rubies in the heavily-hanging trees,/ Broken eyes of queasy cupids staring from the gloom of myrtles./ I came here for solitude/ And I am plucked at by a host of eyes' (*CPW* 474). In 'The Basket' Annette, wanting to be alone, sends her lover, Peter, away; but then, sitting with a basket, she is attacked by 'eyes, hundreds of eyes, round like marbles!/.../ Blue, black, grey, and hazel, and the irises are cased in the whites, and they glitter and spark under the moon./ The basket is heaped with human eyes' (*CPW* 59). Alarmed, Annette flings some of these eyes away and in a macabre image sits and eats the other eyes.

In her 1914 volume, *Sword Blades and Poppy Seeds*, Lowell offered a rebuke to Pound in the poem 'Astigmatism'. The poem is dedicated to Pound 'With Much Friendship and Admiration and Some Differences of Opinion' and turns his visual metaphors against him ('astigmatism' being a term that denotes a defect in the eye or lens that prevents accurate focusing). In the poem Pound is cast as an arrogant poet who wanders through fields of flowers knocking the heads of the blooms with his 'walking-stick/ of fine and polished ebony'. This phallic emblem is used by Lowell to poke fun at Pound's notion of poetry as a pen-craft fit only for men:

> For years the Poet had wrought upon this cane.
> His wealth had gone to enrich it,
> His experiences to pattern it,
> His labour to fashion and burnish it.
> To him it was perfect,
> A work of art and a weapon.
>
> (*CPW* 34)

Bulldozing his way through dahlias and gillyflowers, Pound is unable to see beauty in these flowers, searching zealously only for roses: '"Wretched flowers," said the Poet, "They are not roses"'. The poem addresses the single-minded definition of Imagism proposed by Pound, suggesting that beauty can be found in other flowers than roses, or other forms of Imagism than that espoused by Pound.

In other poems, Lowell shifts attention from the visual to other bodily sensations. 'In Excelsis' renders the sensuality of a possible relationship in ecstatic terms:

> I drink your lips,
> I eat the whiteness of your hands and feet.
> My mouth is open,
> As a new jar I am empty and open.
> Like the white water are you who fill the cup of my mouth,
> Like a brook of water thronged with lilies.
>
> (*CPW* 444)

Here visual contemplation is displaced by the eroticized imagery of eating and drinking, only reappearing in the Imagistic use of simile. The sparse diction follows Imagist doctrine, but the picture of the river suffused with lilies suggests the sensation of the drinking lips rather than their visual design. In 'A Decade', touch is itself replaced by a more highly charged experience:

> When you came, you were like red wine and honey,
> And the taste of you burnt my mouth with its sweetness.
> Now you are like morning bread,
> Smooth and pleasant.
> I hardly taste you at all for I know your savour,
> But I am completely nourished.
>
> (CPW 217)

Here the 'visual concrete' language of one version of Imagism is supplemented with what we might call a 'sensual concrete' discourse: the poem still adheres to a direct presentation of an experience, shuns unnecessary adjectives or superfluous words, and uses simile to compare the lover to a set of physical images of food.

'A Decade' was published in Lowell's volume, *Pictures of the Floating World* (1919), in a sequence of poems, 'Planes of Personality: Two Speak Together'. The series articulated Lowell's love for Ada Russell and is a remarkable example of 'sapphic modernism'.[17] Many of these poems use the symbolism of flowers and other natural elements to voice Lowell's desire for Russell: 'When I think of you, Beloved,/ I see a smooth and stately garden/ With parterres of gold and crimson tulips/ And bursting lilac leaves' (CPW 210). In 'Frimaire', the lovers are 'two flowers/ Blooming last in a yellowing garden,/ A purple aster flower and a red one' (CPW 218). Or again, in 'The Weather-Cock Points South', a poem expressing a barely encoded sexuality:

> I put your leaves aside,
> One by one:
> The stiff, broad outer leaves;
> The smaller ones,
> Pleasant to touch, veined with purple;
> The glazed inner leaves.
> One by one

> I parted you from your leaves,
> Until you stood up like a white flower.
>
> (*CPW* 211)

The exploration of the lover is figured in a highly sensual fashion. As Galvin argues, the depiction of the flower-bud 'is so erotically drawn that it can easily be seen to represent the female genitals, so that this descriptive exploration of the flower is transformed into a celebration of lesbian sexuality'.[18] The language is still Imagistic in its attention to visual detail, the way the small leaves are pleasant to touch and the inner leaves are 'glazed'. Once again, however, visual detail is only a pathway to more sensual pleasures. It might be objected that Lowell's flowery subject matter is arcane, and not in keeping with modernity. But if we view these poems in terms of their lesbian context we can see Lowell re-accentuating jaded images and symbols of femininity with fresh meanings. We might also note that Pound's call for a 'direct treatment of the thing' was somewhat problematic for a poet whose sexual desire could only be voiced *indirectly*.

An illuminating comparison in this respect is to place together two very similar poems by Pound and Lowell. Pound's 'Alba', first published in *The Smart Set* (December 1913), is also a poem employing flower imagery:

> As cool as the pale wet leaves
> of lily-of-the-valley
> She lay beside me in the dawn.
>
> (*IP* 96)

The genre of the 'Alba', dating from the medieval period, is a poem where lovers express regret at the coming of the dawn, whence they must depart. Another form of the poem is the 'Aubade', the title of Lowell's poem, first published in *The Egoist* (February 1914):

> As I would free the white almond from the green husk
> So would I strip our trappings off,
> Beloved.
> And fingering the smooth and polished kernel
> I should see that in my hands glittered a gem beyond counting.
>
> (*CPW* 36)

The proximity of the publication date makes unclear whether Lowell's poem is a direct reply to Pound's, or whether conceived independently.[19] Neither poem follows the genre exactly, since there is no tone of regret at parting here. As well as being more concise, Pound's is the more direct of the two poems, with the final line pointing to a physical relationship: 'She lay beside me'. There is, however, an interesting ambiguity, crystallized in the word 'cool', which though pointing to the feel of the lover's body alongside the protagonist could also refer to a detachment, or cooling off of the lover's relationship. Lowell's poem shows no such indifference, with the simile of the leaves being replaced by a yet more erotic simile, 'fingering' the kernel of the almond. Lowell's poem manages to be not only indirect – she does not say that the lover lies beside her – but also highly sensual, with the focus on the hands touching the lover and with an urgency informing the need to 'strip' the beloved. Lowell's poem represents a desire to tear away external trappings and grasp a hidden 'gem' or essence, a coded plea, perhaps, to openly express her sexuality, and one that echoes the wish to reach beyond the inner leaves of the flower in 'The Weather-Cock Points South'. Both poems are clearly Imagist in form, but also show interesting differences in how the 'treatment of the thing' is articulated. While Pound's 'Alba' retains a sense of distance, Lowell's 'Aubade' reaches across to touch the loved one, recalling the similar haptic desire in H.D.'s 'The Pool'. Like much of H.D.'s verse, 'Aubade' is a poem that crosses a border, from the visual to the tactile, a strategy that symbolizes the transgression of the boundaries of conventional sexuality by these two writers.

At the heart of the modernist project attempted by the Imagists was the notion of 'the image' and in the poetry of H.D. and Lowell we see how the visual basis of the Imagist aesthetic could sometimes be restrictive. However, rather than reject it outright (as Pound thought Lowell had done), these two female poets sought to redefine the 'hard light, clear edges' of Pound's aesthetic and extend Imagism into other varieties of what Lowell termed the 'sensuous sense of seeing'.[20] Lowell's experiments with polyphonic prose, discussed in chapter 5, represent another avenue for such experiments, trying to break free from a univocal viewpoint to allow a plurality of voices and, like much of H.D.'s verse, obliterate boundaries – between prose and poetry, masculine and feminine, homosexual and heterosexual. In this form of Imagism, 'clear edges' are always to be crossed. The distinctive features of the poetry of Lowell and H.D. that have been discussed in this chapter can be connected both to how their identities were formed by membership of the Imagist movement, and also to how they themselves changed the nature of that formation. Polyphony might thus be taken not only as a description of a poetic style, but as an explanation for how the cultural formation itself should be organized. In another sense, the vacillations evident in the poetry of H.D. point to the ambiguous position she occupied within the cultural formation of Imagism. H.D. had been emotionally very close to Pound and was central to his definition of the movement's aesthetic, even though she baulked at being termed an 'Imagiste'. After 1915, however, she shifted allegiance to Lowell's group of poets, a position which Pound, in some ways, viewed as a betrayal, but within which she perhaps felt comfortable because of its commitment to a more polyphonic form of organization. Interpreting H.D. and Lowell in this way is not designed to argue they were somehow not properly Imagist in their verse or that their Imagism was entirely distinct from that of the male members of the group. Rather it is to suggest that our overall understanding of Imagism as a cultural formation changes once the factors of gender and sexuality are read back into the nature of the group and its poetry.

Afterword

In a recent assessment of American modernism Cary Nelson claims that Imagism represents 'a founding movement in modern American poetry that is richer and more diverse than we have been inclined to think'.[1] This book has also stressed the diverse nature of the Imagist movement, drawing attention to figures considered less frequently in conventional literary histories of the group and foregrounding the complex group dynamics and their relation to the wider cultural field of Anglo-American modernism. To conclude, this chapter considers briefly the afterlife of Imagism, assessing its impact upon subsequent modern poetry, after considering the post-Imagist work of some of the key figures in the movement.

The careers of those poets published in the Imagist anthologies of 1914–17 show that the Imagist aesthetic had a profound and enduring effect. Though Pound publicly rejected Imagism after his arguments with Lowell, he continued to employ the method of direct presentation throughout his later poetry, writing in 1927 that the second principle of 'As for Imagisme' ('To use absolutely no word that does not contribute to the presentation') was the key to Imagist verse.[2] Even in the majestic sprawl that is *The Cantos* there are many moments that exemplify this Imagist dictum. One such occurs in the first of the Pisan Cantos, LXXIV, composed in 1945 when Pound was imprisoned in a steel cage near Pisa in Italy, on a charge of treason for radio broadcasts made from Rome during World War II. Pondering his fate and remembering many past events, Pound also writes of what he experiences immediately around him:

> and there was a smell of mint under the tent flaps
> especially after the rain
>   and a white ox on the road toward Pisa
>   as if facing the tower,
> dark sheep in the drill field and on wet days were clouds
> in the mountain as if under the guard roosts.³

The objective presentation of these sights and smells recalls the clarity of images found in 'Ts'ai Chi'h' from *Des Imagistes*, discussed in chapter 4. Here, still, is a direct presentation, with no authorial or subjective comment intervening, and a syntax and vocabulary that remains close to speech. The attention to layout, with the 'white ox' moving across the page to indicate a change in direction of the visual field, perhaps represents a development from Imagism, but even here it is worth recalling the way in which the second line of 'Ts'ai Chi'h' is indented in order to capture the motion of the falling rose petals. The rhythm here clearly owes nothing to the metronome, though we might identify a 'musical phrase' in the repetition of the key conjunctive terms, 'and', 'as if'.

Here Pound does not add anything to explain why he has focused upon these particular images, so the treatment appears wholly objective, though 'the smell of mint' appears later in the canto and is associated with the repeated phrase 'Le Paradis n'est pas artificiel', a reply to Baudelaire's verses praising the idea of an 'artificial paradise'. The 'smell of the mint' can be understood in terms of Pound's theory of the Image in 'A Few Don'ts', where he wrote that the Image was that 'which presents an intellectual and emotional complex in an instant of time'. We might read the initial lines as Pound's immediate emotional response to the beauty of the sights and sounds around him, and its later repetition as the more intellectual part of the 'complex', where he reflects upon the beauty of nature and its rejection by the influential French poet of urban modernity. In 'A Few Don'ts' Pound continued by suggesting that it is 'the presentation of such a "complex" instantaneously which gives that sense of sudden liberation; that sense of freedom from time limits and space limits...which we experience in the presence of the greatest works of art'.⁴ Ironically, Pound's presentation of such paradisiacal yet mundane images of nature allows a metaphorical escape from the limits of time and space at precisely the moment when the poet is most materially bound and constrained in his prison camp. The 'sudden liberation' offered here by the Imagist aesthetic is, for Pound, some small recompense for the state he now finds himself in.

After overseeing the last Imagist anthology, Amy Lowell continued to promote Imagist poetry, or what became known as the 'New Poetry' in America.[5] She also continued to write copiously, publishing works like the experimental *Can Grande's Castle* (1918), comprising four long narrative poems exploring aspects of American history and composed in polyphonic prose.[6] Her interest in Chinese and Japanese poetry, fuelled by her brother Percival's work in Japan in the 1890s, resulted in a collaborative translation with Florence Ayscough of Chinese poetry, entitled *Fir-Flower Tablets* (1921) and a volume of her own verse, *Pictures of the Floating World* (1919), the latter contained 174 short poems, many using the Japanese haiku form.[7] Several other volumes of poetry were published by Lowell, a number posthumously after her death in 1925 at the age of 51. While Pound's work continued to receive much attention, it is only relatively recently that Lowell's poetry has come out of the shadows of 'Amygism'. The publication of a volume of her selected poems in 2002 was the first time for many years that Lowell's work became more readily available.[8]

Other Imagists continued to write much poetry, with H.D.'s being perhaps the most prolific. H.D.'s critical stock has risen since the 1970s, particularly due to the work of many feminist critics who have focused not only on the Imagist period, but also upon her many novels and longer poems.[9] One of the most significant of her later works was *Trilogy*, her response to living in London through the years of World War II. Employing a vast variety of symbols and mythological references *Trilogy* is a complex work, but it still retains the crisp and cryptic quality of H.D.'s best Imagist verse, shown here in an extract whose interrogative mode recalls that of 'The Pool':

> What fruit is our store,
> what flower?
>
> what savour do we possess,
> what particular healing-of-the-nations
>
> is our leaf? Is it balsomodendron,

> herb-basil, or is ours
> the spear and leaf-spire
> of the palm?[10]

While H.D.'s verse might be said to continue and develop the Imagist tradition, others rejected it more strongly. John Gould Fletcher, for example, on returning to America in the 1920s, became associated with the Fugitive group of poets and critics in the southern states, a group who took a critical view of certain forms of modernity and embraced tradition and regionalism. Fletcher, for example, called for a return to classicism and a rejection of Imagism; of the new Fugitive school he wrote:

> It takes the innovations of form of the free-verse school...for granted; what it quarrels with is fundamentally their attitude towards art. It begins by challenging the importance of emotion in poetry; it asserts that intellect and not emotion is the true basis of poetic art; and it proposes a return to classicism as the only possible remedy for the common looseness and facility of much present-day poetic art.[11]

Though, as Richard Gray notes of this comment, it might seem odd to reject Imagism as non-classicist, given that H.D. and Aldington, amongst others, wrote many poems employing classical themes, Fletcher's words suggest a return to poetic *form* as opposed to the perceived emphasis on a *freedom* of expression in Imagism.[12]

If Fletcher and the Fugitive poets took Imagist innovations in one direction, another group developed Imagism in a different mode. This group, again based in America, was that of the Objectivists, first announced in an Objectivist issue of *Poetry* magazine in February 1931, edited by the young Louis Zukofsky. In publishing in *Poetry*, which had been so important for the early dissemination of Imagism, the Objectivists both indicated their mutual heritage and stated that the 'object' had now displaced the 'image' as the watchword for poetry. In fact, the connection was even closer than one of poetic influence, since it was Pound who had recommended Louis Zukofsky to *Poetry*'s editor, Harriet Monroe. Other poets published in the issue included George Oppen, Carl Rakosi, Charles Reznikoff, William Carlos Williams, and Basil Bunting. Although the issue contained two essays by Zukofsky explaining the movement,

'Objectivism' at this point seemed to amount to a restatement of certain Imagist tenets, such as the 'economy of presentation in writing' and the idea of the poem as object.[13] For another contributor to the issue, however, there was a clear demarcation between the two movements. William Carlos Williams, reflecting later upon the period, argued that Imagism had dissipated into mere free verse and had lacked a more programmatic attitude towards verse. Viewing a poem as an object rather than as a collection of images changed the terms of debate considerably, claimed Williams:

> The poem being an object (like a symphony or a cubist painting) it must be the purpose of the poet to make of his words a new form: to invent, that is, an object consonant with his day. This is what we wished to imply by Objectivism, an antidote, in a sense, to the bare image haphazardly presented in loose verse.[14]

Though the two movements are distinguished sharply in such claims, their common lineage is still evident. It was Pound, after all, who had written to Harriet Monroe in 1915 calling for a poetry that exemplified 'Objectivity and again objectivity' since 'language is made out of concrete things'.[15] Likewise we might note that the aim of poets like Lowell, Fletcher, and Flint was always to write in a form of verse 'consonant' with their times.

Without collapsing Objectivism completely into Imagism, it is worth noting the influence of certain Imagist strategies in the later poetic. A poem by George Oppen, 'Bad Times', from his 1934 volume *Discrete Series*, published by the Objectivist Press, indicates some of these similarities:

> Bad times:
> The cars pass
> By the elevated posts
> And the movie sign.
> A man sells post-cards.

Knowing of Oppen's membership of the Communist Party, we are alerted to the implied social critique in the poem, where the only human being in the poem is defined by their trivial occupation. Formally, however, what is interesting is the use of the colon after the first line: this is the technique of the suppressed simile, so favoured by Imagism, such as in the two lines of Pound's 'Metro' poem. The technique was informed by

Hulme's claim that thought consists of the simultaneous presentation of two different images, and in Pound's poem we are meant to see the petals on the wet, black bough as *like* the faces in the underground. The difference in Oppen's poem is that the 'Bad times' described after the colon are not to be viewed as *like* this, rather they *are* this. Inserting the words 'are like' after Oppen's opening line ('Bad times are like') makes little sense; whereas if the same words are placed at the end of the first line of 'In a Station of the Metro', they clarify the poem considerably. This kind of approach to the reality of experience, of course, might still be indebted to Pound's 'direct presentation of the thing', but there does seem to be some difference here, with a heightened concern for facticity and sincerity (a key Objectivist term for Zukofsky) being manifest in Oppen. In Oppen's own words, 'What I felt I was doing was beginning from imagism as a position of honesty'.[16]

What most clearly emerges as the legacy of Imagism for American verse – and the British case does seem to differ here – is the continuing tradition of experimenting with poetic form. While much British poetry of the twenties and thirties retreated into stricter metrical forms, many American poets followed Williams in believing that the poet had almost a duty to innovate in terms of their form. A concern for formal experimentation can be traced from Imagism, via Objectivism, up to Charles Olson's 'Projective Verse' and the Black Mountain Group, and into the latter part of the twentieth century with the LANGUAGE poets. For example, Olson's 'kinetics of the thing' recalls Williams's claim that in poetry there are 'no ideas but in things',[17] a position informed in turn by Pound's letter in 1908 to Williams asserting that a central aim for poetry was 'To paint the thing as I see it'. It was a point of view that Pound repeated to Williams more emphatically again in 1920: 'When did I ever, in enmity, advise you to use vague words, to shun the welding of word and thing, to avoid hard statement, word close to the thing it means?'[18] These joint concerns – towards formal experimentation and a concern for a verse rooted in the concrete or things – informs much twentieth-century American verse and may be said to be Imagism's most profound legacy for poetry.

Though a critic like Richard Gray suggests that an 'observation of the concrete' is what typifies modern American verse from Imagism onwards,[19] it should be remembered that it was the English philosopher T. E. Hulme who most profoundly theorized the importance of a 'thingly' epistemology for poetry, as discussed in chapter 4. In the *Cantos*, too, Pound also credited the influence of another English writer, Ford Madox Ford, for his 'conversation was better,/ consisting in *res* non *verba*', words rather than things.[20]

Aside from matters of formal influence, however, what was suggested by Imagism was the importance of conceiving of poetry in terms of a movement, or what has been called here a cultural formation, the practices of which have been analysed in chapters 1 to 3. Numerous groupings in American poetry, from Objectivism onwards, have embraced the Imagist approach to the promotion of poetry; that is, the idea of a movement, an ism, a manifesto or critical statement of aims, and alternative means of publication, often that of the 'little magazine'. This process of cultural production, prompted by an awareness of how the cultural marketplace for poetry operated in the twentieth century, was understood first of all by Imagism, and in particular by its two central protagonists, Pound and Lowell. Such an understanding of how poetry operates within the wider conditions of modernity, along with the stress upon formal experimentation, attention to the concrete, and precision of language, are the true legacies of the Imagist movement. For these reasons alone – and of course for the many incisive poems they produced – Imagist poetry is still worthy of further attention.

Notes

INTRODUCTION: THE FORMATION OF IMAGISM

1. T. S. Eliot, 'American Literature and the American Language', cited in Peter Jones (ed.), *Imagist Poetry* (Harmondsworth: Penguin, 1972), 14. C. K. Stead's *The New Poetic: Yeats to Eliot* (Harmondsworth: Penguin, 1967) is a good example of the traditional view of Imagism taken by literary history.
2. The term 'cultural formation' was coined by Raymond Williams. For an explanation and discussion of the term see David Peters Corbett and Andrew Thacker, 'Cultural Formations in Modernism: Movements and Magazines 1890–1920', *Prose Studies,* 16:2 (August 1993), 84–106.
3. Lawrence Rainey, *Institutions of Modernism: Literary Elites and Public Culture* (New Haven/London: Yale University Press, 1998), 31.
4. For information see *The Letters of D. H. Lawrence and Amy Lowell 1914–1925*, ed. E. Claire Healey and Keith Cushman (Santa Barbara: Black Sparrow Press, 1985).
5. Richard Aldington, *Life for Life's Sake* (London: Cassell and Co, 1969), 130–31.
6. Amy Lowell, Letter to Harriet Monroe, 15 September 1914, cited in Gillian Hanscombe and Virginia L. Smyers, *Writing for their Lives: The Modernist Woman 1910–1940* (London: Women's Press, 1987), 200–201.
7. Ezra Pound, *The Selected Letters of Ezra Pound, 1907–1941*, ed. D. D. Paige (London: Faber, 1950), 38.
8. Pound, *Selected Letters*, 48.
9. Richard Le Gallienne, 'Sunset in the City', in his *English Poems* (London: John Lane, 1895), 89.
10. For the influence of France see Cyrena N. Pondrom, *The Road from Paris: French Influence on English Poetry, 1900–1920* (Cambridge: Cambridge University Press, 1974).

CHAPTER 1. MOVEMENTS AND MODERNISM

1. The poems included 'Hermes of the Ways', 'Priapus', and 'Epigram'. For H.D.'s account of this event see H.D., *End to Torment; A Memoir of Ezra Pound by H.D.*, ed. Norman Holmes Pearson and Michael King (Manchester: Carcanet, 1980), 18.
2. Richard Aldington, *Life for Life's Sake* (London: Cassell and Co, 1969), 123.
3. See Letter quoted in Le Roy C. Breunig, 'F. S. Flint, Imagism's Maitre D'Ecole', *Comparative Literature*, 4:2 (Spring 1952), 134.
4. Pound, 'Prefatory Note to "The Complete Poems of T. E. Hulme"', in his *Ripostes* volume of 1912; *Collected Shorter Poems* (London: Faber, 1984), 251. For more information on these two groups see Robert Ferguson, *The Short Sharp Life of T. E. Hulme* (London: Allen Lane, 2002), ch.3. For an account of the role of venues for modernist meetings, such as restaurants and cafés, see Peter Brooker, *Bohemia in London: The Social Scene of Early Modernism* (Basingstoke: Palgrave, 2004).
5. F. S. Flint, 'Lecture 1940', cited in J. B. Harmer, *Victory in Limbo: Imagism 1908–1917* (London: Secker and Warburg, 1975), 17.
6. Douglas Goldring, *South Lodge: Reminiscences of Violet Hunt, Ford Madox Ford and the 'English Review' Circle* (London: Constable, 1943), 62.
7. For some sense of the range of such movements see Lawrence Rainey, *Modernism: An Anthology* (Oxford: Blackwell, 2005).
8. Ford Madox Ford, 'Those Were the Days', in *Imagist Anthology 1930* (London: Chatto and Windus, 1930), ix.
9. It should be said that the distinction is not always that clear, with Pound insisting that Imagism was the literary form of Vorticism. The restaurant in the painting, the *Tour Eiffel*, did function as an important meeting place for the Imagists.
10. See T. W. Heyck, *The Transformation of Intellectual Life in Victorian England* (London: Croom Helm, 1982); for the now classic account of this high/low divide in modernism see Andreas Huyssens, *After the Great Divide: Modernism, Mass Culture, Postmodernism* (Bloomington: Indiana University Press, 1986).
11. George Gissing, *New Grub Street* (Harmondsworth: Penguin, 1985), 81.
12. Ibid.,150.
13. Ibid., 38.
14. See Michael North, *Reading 1922: A Return to the Scene of the Modern* (Oxford: Oxford University Press, 1999); Mark Morrisson, *The Public Face of Modernism: Little Magazines, Audiences, and Reception 1905–*

1920 (Madison: University of Wisconsin Press, 2001); and Lawrence Rainey, *Institutions of Modernism: Literary Elites and Public Culture* (New Haven/London: Yale University Press, 1998).
15. Morrisson, *Public Face of Modernism*, 6.
16. See, for example, the comments, 'AUTOMOBILISM (Marinettism) bores us' and 'The futurist is a sensational and sentimental mixture of the aesthete of 1890 and the realist of 1870'; see 'Long Live the Vortex!', *Blast*, 1 (1914).
17. 'A Few Don'ts by an Imagiste', in *Imagist Poetry*, ed. Peter Jones (Harmondsworth: Penguin, 1972), 132.
18. *Pound/Joyce: The Letters of Ezra Pound to James Joyce, with Pound's Essays on Joyce*, ed. Forrest Read (New York: New Directions, 1967), 18.
19. Pound, no date; cited in Helen Carr, *The Verse Revolutionaries: Ezra Pound, H.D. and the Imagists* (London: Jonathan Cape, 2009), 89.
20. Joy Grant, *Harold Monro and the Poetry Bookshop* (London: Routledge and Kegan Paul, 1967), 96. For an account of the Georgians see Rennie Parker, *The Georgian Poets* (Plymouth: Northcote House, 1998).
21. Aldington, *Life for Life's Sake*, 100.
22. Cited in Noel Stock, *The Life of Ezra Pound* (Harmondsworth: Penguin Books, 1974), 175.
23. Cited in Charles Doyle, *Richard Aldington: A Biography* (London: Macmillan, 1989), 30.
24. Breunig, 'F.S. Flint', 120–21.
25. Joy Grant, *Harold Monro and the Poetry Bookshop*, 54.
26. Rainey, *Institutions of Modernism*, 30.
27. Ibid., 38.
28. Ibid., 30.
29. See Pound, 'Imagisme', in *Imagist Poetry*, 129.
30. Aldington, *Life for Life's Sake*, 121.
31. Amy Lowell, *Tendencies in Modern American Poetry* (Boston: Houghton Mifflin, 1917), 235, 237.
32. See Raymond Williams, *Culture* (London: Fontana, 1981), 68–71.
33. Harold Monro, *Poetry and Drama* (June 1913), 12.
34. Ezra Pound, 'Status Rerum – the Sacred', *Poetry*, 8 (April 1916), 41.
35. For a discussion of Lowell's body see Melissa Bradshaw, 'Remembering Amy Lowell', in Adrienne Munich and Melissa Bradshaw (eds.), *Amy Lowell: American Modern* (New Brunswick: Rutgers University Press, 2004).
36. For a commentary upon the various contemporary memoirs of the Lowell/Pound dispute, especially the two eventful dinners in 1914, see Brooker, *Bohemia in London*, 114–21.
37. Aldington, *Life for Life's Sake*, 127.

38. Pound, *Selected Letters 1907–1941*, ed. D. D. Paige, (London: Faber, 1950), 48.
39. Pound, 'The New Sculpture', *Egoist* (February 1914), 68.
40. Lowell, Letter, 3 November 1914, cited in Claire Healey, 'Amy Lowell Visits London', *New England Quarterly*, 46:3 (September 1973), 448.
41. Lowell, letter, 15 September 1914, in *Dear Editor: A History of 'Poetry' in Letters – The First Fifty Years*, ed. Joseph Parisi and Stephen Young, (New York, Norton, 2002), 159.
42. Pound, *Selected Letters*, 38.
43. Aldington, *Life for Life's Sake*, 121.
44. Cited in Jean Gould, *Amy: The World of Amy Lowell and the Imagist Movement* (New York: Dodd, Mead and Co, 1975), 353.
45. T. S. Eliot, cited in *Selected Poems of Amy Lowell*, ed. Melissa Bradshaw and Adrienne Munich (New Brunswick: Rutgers University Press, 2002), xv.
46. See Gould, Amy, 176; S. Foster Damon, *Amy Lowell: A Chronicle* (Boston and New York: Houghton Mifflin, 1935), 368.
47. For information see *The Letters of D. H. Lawrence and Amy Lowell 1914–1925*, ed. E. Claire Healey and Keith Cushman (Santa Barbara: Black Sparrow Press, 1985). Lowell's own poetry also sold well, with *Legends* (1921) selling 2,000 copies within three weeks.
48. Quoted in Jayne E. Marek, 'Amy Lowell, *Some Imagist Poets*, and the Context of the New Poetry' in Munich and Bradshaw (eds.), *American Modern*, 164.
49. See Foster Damon, *Amy Lowell*, 613.
50. Marek, 'Amy Lowell', 164.

CHAPTER 2. PUBLISHING, PUBLICITY, AND MAGAZINES

1. Richard Ellmann, *Golden Codgers* (Oxford: Oxford University Press, 1973), 101.
2. Peter McDonald, 'Modernist Publishing', in David Bradshaw (ed.), *A Concise Companion to Modernism* (Oxford: Blackwell, 2003), 241. The whole of this chapter is a fascinating consideration of the publication history of Pound's 'In a Station of the Metro'.
3. Ezra Pound, 'Small Magazines', *English Journal*, 19:9 (November 1930), 702.
4. Frederick J. Hoffman, Charles Allen and Carolyn F. Ulrich, *The Little Magazine: A History and a Bibliography* (New Jersey: Princeton University Press, 1947), 2–3. For a recent assessment of the 'little magazine' see Peter Brooker and Andrew Thacker (eds.) *The Oxford Critical and Cultural History of Modernist Magazines. Volume 1; Britain*

and Ireland, 1880–1955 (Oxford: Oxford University Press, 2009).
5. Mark Morrisson, *The Public Face of Modernism: Little Magazines, Audiences, and Reception 1905–1920* (Madison: University of Wisconsin Press, 2001), 10–11.
6. Hoffman gives a 'conservative estimate' of over 600 magazines published in English since 1912. Starting earlier, in the 1880s, increases the total, and the addition of non-Anglophone European modernist magazines only adds to this number.
7. Hugh Kenner, *The Pound Era* (Berkeley/Los Angeles: University of California Press, 1971), 279.
8. See, inter alia, Jean-Michel Rabaté, 'Joyce the Egoist', *Modernism/Modernity*, 4:3 (September 1997), 45–66; Bruce Clarke, *Dora Marsden and Early Modernism: Gender, Individualism, Science* (Ann Arbor: University of Michigan Press, 1996); Robert von Hallberg, 'Libertarian Imagism', *Modernism/Modernity*, no.2 (April 1995), 63–79.
9. Marsden, 'Bondwomen', *The Freewoman*, 23 November 1911, 3.
10. Morrisson, *Public Face of Modernism*, 91.
11. Ibid., 92.
12. Cited in Carol Barash, 'Dora Marsden's Feminism, *The Freewoman* and the Gender Politics of Early Modernism', *Princeton University Library Chronicle*, Winter 1987, 46.
13. Cited in Gillian Hanscombe and Virginia L. Smyers, *Writing for their Lives: The Modernist Woman 1910–1940* (London: Women's Press, 1987), 165.
14. Advertising flyer, no date, Harriet Shaw Weaver papers, British Library, mss 57355.
15. See, for example, Michael H. Levenson, *A Genealogy of Modernism: A Study of English Literary Doctrine 1908–1922* (Cambridge: Cambridge University Press, 1984), 63–79.
16. Marsden, *New Freewoman* (15 June 1913), 3; (15 October 1913), 165.
17. Pound, 'Imagisme', in *Imagist Poetry*, 129.
18. Pound, *Selected Letters 1907–1941*, ed. D. D. Paige (London: Faber, 1950), 22.
19. Letter, *New Freewoman*, (15 December 1913), 244.
20. See K. K. Ruthven, 'Ezra's Appropriations', *Times Literary Supplement*, 20–26 November 1987, 1300.
21. See Les Garner, *A Brave and Beautiful Spirit: Dora Marsden, 1882–1960* (Avebury: Gower Publishing, 1990), 118.
22. Joy Grant, *Harold Monro and the Poetry Bookshop*, 54.
23. Cited in John Gould Fletcher, *Life Is My Song* (New York/Toronto: Farrar and Rinehart, 1937), 63. See Morrisson, *Public Face of Modernism*, 102.
24. 'Bastien von Helmholtz', 'Poetry', *The Egoist* (1 June 1914), 215.
25. Pound, *Literary Essays*, ed. T. S. Eliot (London: Faber, 1954), 221.

26. Fletcher, *Life Is My Song*, 62. The date Fletcher gives for offering to help the *English Review* is 1911, but given that Ford stopped editing the magazine in December 1909, this seems an error.
27. See Fletcher, letter, 7 September 1913, *Selected Letters*, ed. Leighton Rudolph, Lucas Carpenter and Ethel C. Simpson (Fayetteville: University of Arkansas Press, 1996), 3.
28. Fletcher, *Selected Letters*, 3. P. T. Barnum (1810–91) was a famous American impresario, promoter, and circus founder.
29. Fletcher, *Life Is My Song*, 127.
30. Pound, *Selected Letters*, 31.
31. Ibid., 34.
32. Pound, *The Letters of Ezra Pound to Margaret Anderson: The Little Review Correspondence*, ed. Thomas L. Scott and Melvin J. Frieman (New York: New Directions, 1988), 178.
33. Cited in Melissa Bradshaw, 'Outselling the Modernisms of Men: Amy Lowell and the Art of Self-Commodification', *Victorian Poetry*, 38:1 (2000), 142.
34. Pound to Harriet Monroe, 15 September 1914, cited in *Florence Ayscough and Amy Lowell: Correspondence of a Friendship*, ed. Harley Farnsworth MacNair (Chicago: University of Chicago Press, 1945), 253.
35. Jayne E. Marek, 'Amy Lowell, *Some Imagist Poets*, and the Context of the New Poetry', in Adrienne Munich and Melissa Bradshaw (eds.), *Amy Lowell: American Modern* (New Brunswick: Rutgers University Press, 2004), 156. According to Fletcher, however, Lowell continued to think of starting a monthly magazine as late as Christmas 1915, with Aldington as editor (Fletcher, *Selected Letters*, 37).
36. See Ellery Sedgwick III, ' "Fireworks": Amy Lowell and the *Atlantic Monthly*', *New England Quarterly*, 51:4 (December 1978), 489–508.
37. Cited in Marek, 'Amy Lowell', 158.
38. Marek, 'Amy Lowell', 160.
39. See Marek, 'Amy Lowell', 160.
40. Marsden, 'Women's Rights', *The Egoist* (1 October 1914), 361.

CHAPTER 3. PREFACES AND MANIFESTOS

1. See Pound's reference to them in his 'A Retrospect' of 1918; see Pound, *Literary Essays*, 3–14.
2. Edmund De Chasca, *John Gould Fletcher and Imagism* (Columbia: University of Missouri Press, 1978), 19.
3. *Georgian Poetry, 1911–12* (London: Poetry Bookshop, 1912), Prefatory Note.
4. F. Marinetti, 'The Founding and Manifesto of Futurism 1909', in

Futurist Manifestos, ed. Umbro Apollonia, (London: Thames and Hudson, 1973), 21.
5. Cited in Walter Michel and C. J. Fox (eds.), *Wyndham Lewis on Art: Collected Writings, 1913–1956* (New York: Funk and Wagnalls, 1969), 58.
6. Janet Lyon, *Manifestos: Provocations of the Modern* (Ithaca and London: Cornell University Press, 1999), 5.
7. Ibid., 128.
8. Ibid., 129.
9. Ibid., 134–5.
10. Fletcher, *Selected Letters*, 2.
11. Pound, *Selected Letters*, 213.
12. Cited in Helen Carr, *The Verse Revolutionaries: Ezra Pound, H.D. and the Imagists* (London: Jonathan Cape, 2009), 538.
13. Pound's note to 'The Complete Poetical Works of T. E. Hulme', first published in his volume *Ripostes* (1912); see Pound, *Collected Shorter Poems* (London: Faber, 1984), 251.
14. For the impact of this exhibition see Peter Stansky, *On or About December 1910: Early Bloomsbury and Its Intimate World* (Cambridge, MA: Harvard University Press, 1997).
15. F. S. Flint, 'History of Imagism', *Egoist*, (1 May 1915), 71.
16. See Le Roy C. Breunig, 'F. S. Flint, Imagism's "Maitre D'Ecole"', *Comparative Literature*, 4:2 (Spring 1952), 134.
17. Pound, letter to Margaret Anderson, 17 November 1917, cited in Harmer, *Victory in Limbo*, 214. Pound called Flint's history 'bullshit' in a letter to him, 2 July 1915.
18. Schwartz traces this point to Remy de Gourmont; see Sanford Schwartz, *The Matrix Of Modernism: Pound, Eliot, and Early Twentieth Century Thought* (Princeton, NJ: Princeton University Press, 1985), 57.
19. See Wallace Martin, 'The Sources of the Imagist Aesthetic', *PMLA*, 85 (1970), 180.
20. Henri Bergson, *An Introduction to Metaphysics* (1903; trans. T. E. Hulme, London: Macmillan, 1913), 14. In *Matter and Memory* (New York: Zone Books, 1991) Bergson suggests that matter is 'an aggregate of "images"' (p. 9).
21. Raymond Williams, *The Politics of Modernism: Against the New Conformists* (London: Verso, 1989), 73–7.
22. H.D. 'The Pool', *Poetry*, 5:6 (March 1915), 266.
23. Pound, *Selected Letters*, 213.
24. May Sinclair, 'Two Notes', *Egoist*, (1 May 1915), 88–9.
25. Hulme, cited in Alan Jones, *The Life and Opinions of T. E. Hulme* (London: Gollancz, 1960), 211.
26. Rainer Emig, *Modernism in Poetry: Motivations, Structures and Limits*

(London: Longman, 1995), 107.
27. Pound, *Selected Letters*, 49.
28. The relation between the French *vers libre* and the Anglicized 'free verse' is very complex. The former could include the use of end-rhymes, a feature not normally associated with 'free verse' in English. For an extended discussion on the relation between the two see Cyrena Pondrom, *The Road from Paris: French Influence on English Poetry, 1900–1920* (Cambridge: Cambridge University Press, 1974).
29. See Hanscombe and Smyers, *Writing for their Lives*, 200.
30. Cited in Marek, 'Amy Lowell', 158.
31. Aldington's mark upon the preface is noticeable if one compares his June 1914 article on Imagism in *The Egoist*, which contains a number of very similar comments, including six key principles for Imagist poetry.
32. Pound, *Selected Letters*, 48. Pound argued that Ford's insistence upon the use of 'simple speech' dated back to their first meetings in 1908.
33. See Marek, 'Amy Lowell', 161.
34. Florence Farr, *The Music of Speech, Containing the Words of Some Poets, Thinkers and Music-Makers Regarding the Practice of the Bardic Art Together with Fragments of Verse Set to its Own Melody* (London: Elkin Matthews, 1909), 19.
35. Farr, *Music of Speech*, 5, 11.
36. Cited in Noel Stock, *The Life of Ezra Pound* (Harmondsworth: Penguin, 1970), 92.
37. Pound, *Literary Essays*, 437. Pound's interest in the links between music and poetry are also found in his work with the composer Walter Rummel, with whom he stayed briefly in Paris in 1911.
38. See *Selected Poems of Amy Lowell*, pp. xix–xx, for accounts of her recitals.
39. For information on her friendship with the French-trained composer Carl Engel see Jean Gould, *Amy: The World of Amy Lowell and the Imagist Movement* (New York: Dodd, Mead and Co., 1975), 84–91.
40. Lucas Carpenter, *John Gould Fletcher and Southern Modernism* (Lafayette/London: University of Arkansas Press, 1990), 115.
41. John Gould Fletcher, 'Miss Lowell's Discovery: Polyphonic Prose' *Poetry*, 6 (April 1915), 35.
42. John Gould Fletcher, *Life Is My Song* (New York and Toronto: Farrar and Rinehart, 1937), 201.
43. For a brief overview of the rise of prose poetry in European modernism see Clive Scott, 'The Prose Poem and Free Verse', in Malcolm Bradbury and James McFarlane (eds.), *Modernism: A Guide*

    to European Literature 1890–1930 (Harmondsworth: Penguin, 1976).
44. Amy Lowell, *Sword Blades and Poppy Seeds* (London: Macmillan, 1914), x–xi.
45. Amy Lowell, 'Some Musical Analogies in Modern Poetry', *Musical Quarterly*, January 1920, cited in S. Foster Damon, *Amy Lowell: A Chronicle With Extracts From Her Correspondence* (Boston and New York: Houghton Mifflin, 1935), 471.
46. Lowell, 'Some Musical Analogies', cited in Damon, *Amy Lowell*, 471.
47. See Mikhail Bakhtin, *Problems of Dostoevsky's Poetics*, trans. Caryl Emerson (Manchester: Manchester University Press, 1984).
48. *Des Imagistes* had included John Cournos's short prose poem, 'The Rose', and in this period other writers published a number of prose poems, such as T. S. Eliot's 'Hysteria', in Pound's *Catholic Anthology* (1915) and Gertrude Stein's *Tender Buttons*, composed in 1911 and published in 1914. Lowell, however, is alone amongst modernist writers in providing such a systematic and theoretical attempt to utilize prose for poetic purposes.

CHAPTER 4. MODERN THEMES

1. Pound, *Selected Letters*, 49.
2. Richard Aldington, 'Modern Poetry and the Imagists', *Egoist* (1 June 1914), 202.
3. John T. Gage, *In the Arresting Eye: The Rhetoric of Imagism* (Baton Rouge: Louisiana State University Press, 1981), 64.
4. Pound, 'The Encounter', first published in *Smart Set* (December 1913); see *Collected Shorter Poems* (London: Faber, 1968), 110.
5. Ezra Pound, 'Vorticism' (1914), reproduced in *Gaudier-Brzeska: A Memoir* (1916; repr. New York: New Directions, 1970), 88.
6. Ruthven argues that the 'new morality' refers to the recently translated work of Freud; see K. K. Ruthven, *A Guide to Ezra Pound's 'Personae'* (1926) (Berkeley: University of California Press, 1969), 63.
7. Eliot, 'Introduction' to Ezra Pound, *Selected Poems* (London: Faber, 1928), xvi.
8. Pound, *Collected Shorter Poems*, 94.
9. Pound, *Selected Letters*, 25.
10. Helen Carr, 'Imagism and Empire', in H. Booth and N. Rigby (eds.), *Modernism and Empire* (Manchester: Manchester University Press, 2000), 66.
11. Zhaoming Qian, *Orientalism and Modernism: The Legacy of China in Pound and Williams* (Durham: Duke University Press, 1995), 5. Qian uses Orientalism differently from Said, specifically to refer to visual and literary culture freed from the usual matrix of power-knowl-

edge.
12. The notion of a cultural contact zone derives from Mary Louis Pratt in *Imperial Eyes: Travel and Transculturation* (London: Routledge, 1992) and has been applied for exhibition culture by James Clifford in his *Routes: Travel and Translation in the Late Twentieth Century* (Cambridge, MA: Harvard University Press, 1997).
13. Qian, *Orientalism and Modernism*, 43–6.
14. Ibid., 45.
15. Quoted in Qian, *Orientalism and Modernism*, 45.
16. Qian, *Orientalism and Modernism*, 46.
17. Flint 'The History of Imagism', *Egoist* (1 May 1915), 70–71.
18. For more on this see Andrew Thacker, ' "Mad After Foreign Notions": Ezra Pound, Imagism and the Geography of the Orient', in Peter Brooker and Andrew Thacker (eds.), *Geographies of Modernsim: Literatures, Cultures, Spaces* (Abingdon: Routledge, 2005).
19. Yone Noguchi, 'What is a Hokku Poem?' *Rhythm*, 12 (January 1913), 354–9.
20. See James G. Nelson, *Elkin Matthews: Publisher to Yeats, Joyce, Pound* (Madison: Wisconsin University Press, 1989), 152.
21. For a discussion of the possible impact of Noguchi's work upon Pound see Y. Hakutani (ed.), *Selected Writings of Yone Noguchi: An East-West Literary Assimilation*, vol.2, *Prose* (London and Toronto: Fairleigh Dickinson University Press, 1992). Interestingly, Bob Blaisdell's *Imagist Poetry: An Anthology* (New York: Dover Publications, 1999) includes Noguchi's 'I Have Cast the World'.
22. S. Kodama (ed.), *Ezra Pound and Japan: Letters and Essays* (Redding Ridge, CT: Black Swan Books, 1987), 5.
23. Laurence Binyon, *Painting in the Far East: An Introduction to the History of Pictorial Art in Asia, Especially China and India* (London: Edward Arnold, 1908), 5.
24. Binyon, *Painting in the Far East*, 6.
25. Pound, Preface to 'F.T.S.', 'The Causes and Remedy of the Poverty of China', *Egoist* (16 March 1914), 105.
26. Ernest Fenollosa *The Chinese Written Character as a Medium for Poetry*, ed. Ezra Pound (San Francisco: City Lights, 1969) 4.
27. Rainey, *Institutions of Modernism*, 15.
28. *Ezra Pound and Dorothy Shakespeare: Their Letters: 1909–1914*, ed. O. Pound and A. Walton Litz (London: Faber, 1985), 267.
29. Pound, 'Affirmations', *New Age*, 14 January 1915, 277–8.
30. *Ezra Pound and Dorothy Shakespeare*, 264. Pound, according to Wilhelm, used to visit a Chinese restaurant in Regent Street around 1913–14; see J. J. Wilhelm, *Ezra Pound in London and Paris 1908–1925* (Philadelphia: Penn State University Press, 1990) 132.
31. Kodama, *Ezra Pound and Japan*, 201.

32. Percival Lowell also published a number of books of travel writing about Japan, such as *The Soul of the Far East* (1888).
33. Amy Lowell, *Can Grande's Castle* (Boston: Houghton Mifflin, 1918), xvi.
34. See Mari Yoshihara, 'Putting on the Voice of the Orient: Gender and Sexuality in Amy Lowell's "Asian" Poetry', in Munich and Bradshaw (eds.), *Amy Lowell, American Modern*.
35. Fletcher, *Life Is My Song*, 185.
36. See Helen Carr, 'Imagism and Empire'.

CHAPTER 5. URBAN IMAGES

1. Hugh Kenner, *The Pound Era* (London: Pimlico, 1991), 184.
2. For a more detailed account of Pound's poem in the context of underground railways see ch. 3, 'Imagist Travels' of my *Moving Through Modernity*.
3. Richard Aldington, 'In the Tube', *The Complete Poems of Richard Aldington* (London: Allen Wingate, 1948), 49. The poem was first published in *The Egoist* (1 March 1915).
4. Ezra Pound, 'Vorticism' (1914); reprinted in Pound, *Gaudier-Brzeska: A Memoir* (New York: New Directions, 1970), 86–7. The Paris Metro had first opened in 1900 and La Concorde station was, and is still, upon one of the original lines of the network.
5. Georg Simmel, 'Soziologie des Raumes', cited in Walter Benjamin, *Charles Baudelaire: A Lyric Poet in the Era of High Capitalism* (London: Verso, 1983) 37–8.
6. Elizabeth Wilson, *The Sphinx in the City Urban Life, the Control of Disorder, and Women* (London: Virago, 1991), 24.
7. Richard Aldington, 'The Poetry of F. S. Flint', *The Egoist* (1 May 1915), 81.
8. Pound, *Collected Shorter Poems*, 74.
9. Suzanne Churchill notes that William Carlos Williams first eliminated initial letters in a set of poems published in *Others* magazine for February 1916 – almost two years after Flint's use of the technique. See Suzanne W. Churchill, *The Little Magazine 'Others' and the Renovation of Modern American Poetry* (Aldershot: Ashgate, 2006), 108.
10. For a discussion of this, with particular relation to H.D., see Trudi Tate, *Modernism, History and the First World War* (Manchester: Manchester University Press, 1998), ch. 1, 'War Neuroses'.
11. H.D., *Bid Me to Live* (London: Virago, 1984), 109.
12. Fletcher, *Life Is My Song*, 42.
13. Ibid., 53.

14. John Gould Fletcher, 'The Hoardings', in *The Dominant City (1911–12)* (London: Max Goshen, 1913), 7.
15. Elizabeth Wilson, *Hallucinations: Life in the Postmodern City* (London: Radius Hutchinson, 1988), 167.
16. Harold Monro, 'The Imagists Discussed', *The Egoist* (1 May 1915), 79.
17. Ibid.
18. Bryony Randall, 'John Gould Fletcher's City Aesthetic: "London Excursion"', *Literary London*, 4:1 (2006), 7, www.literarylondon.org/london-journal/randall.html.
19. Fletcher, *Life Is My Song*, 92–3.
20. The setting of the poem seems to refer to Lowell's home in Brookline, a suburb of the city of Boston.
21. Amy Lowell, *Can Grande's Castle* (Boston: Houghton Mifflin, 1918), xiv.
22. A point made by Lowell in *Tendencies in American Poetry* (Boston and New York: Houghton Mifflin, 1917), 244.
23. Eliot, cited in Lyndall Gordon, *Eliot's Early Years* (Oxford: Oxford University Press, 1977), 108. Interestingly, Lowell's other contribution to the 1916 Imagist anthology was a poem that tried to reproduce the 'sound and movement' of a string quartet by the same composer.
24. See Pound, *Gaudier-Brzeska*, 90.
25. Williams, *The Politics of Modernism*, 46.
26. Amy Lowell, *Men, Women and Ghosts* (Boston and New York: Houghton Mifflin, 1916), x–xi.
27. Ibid., xi.
28. Bryher, *Amy Lowell: A Critical Appreciation* (London: Eyre and Spottiswoode, 2nd edn, 1918), 32.
29. Ibid.
30. Virginia Woolf, 'Modern Fiction', in *The Crowded Dance of Modern Life: Selected Essays*, vol. 2, ed. Rachel Bowlby (Harmondsworth: Penguin, 1993), 10.
31. Bryher, *Amy Lowell*, 33.
32. Ibid.
33. For an overview of debates around modernist women writers and the *flâneur* see Deborah L. Parsons, *Streetwalking the City: Women, the City and Modernity* (Oxford: Oxford University Press, 2000).
34. Lowell, *Men, Women and Ghosts*, x.
35. Fredric Jameson, *The Political Unconscious: Narrative as a Socially Symbolic Act* (London: Methuen, 1981), 63.
36. Lowell, *Men, Women and Ghosts*, 358.

CHAPTER 6. GENDER AND SEXUALITY: 'AMYGISM' AND 'H.D. IMAGISTE'

1. No attention to such issues is found in standard accounts of Imagism such as that of Harmer (1975) or Gage (1981).
2. Pound, 'Status Rerum – The Sacred', *Poetry*, 8 April 1916, 41; *Selected Letters*, 114.
3. Cyrena Pondrom, 'H.D. and the Origins of Imagism', in Susan Stanford Friedman and Rachel Blau DuPlessis (eds.), *Signets: Reading H.D.* (Madison: University of Wisconsin Press, 1990), 86.
4. See also Hulme's comments on the 'two tarts walking down Piccadilly on tiptoe' (SW 42).
5. For an interesting defence and revision of classicism in Hulme see Edward P. Comentale, *Modernism, Cultural Production, and the British Avant-Garde* (Cambridge: Cambridge University Press, 2004), 17–25 and 113–50.
6. Reading Ferguson's recent biography clearly reveals Hulme's very traditional view of the roles he expected for women, especially those of his lover Kate Lechmere; see Robert Ferguson, *The Short Sharp Life of T. E. Hulme* (London: Allen Lane, 2002).
7. Richard Aldington, 'Modern Poetry and the Imagists', *Egoist* (1 June 1914), 202.
8. Pound, *Selected Letters*, 38.
9. For H.D.'s account of this see her *End to Torment: A Memoir of Ezra Pound* (Manchester: Carcanet, 1980), 18.
10. Edmund De Chasca, *John Gould Fletcher and Imagism* (Columbia: University of Missouri Press, 1978), 18.
11. Richard Aldington, *Medallions* (London: Chatto and Windus, 1930), 9.
12. For example, Clare Buck notes how H.D.'s early poetry 'characteristically represents not one but two realities' (Clare Buck, *H.D. and Freud: Bisexuality and a Feminine Discourse*, Hemel Hempstead: Harvester Wheatsheaf, 1991, 23), while Gary Burnett notes how her verse explores 'a land of boundaries and difficult juxtapositions' (Gary Burnett, *H.D. Between Image and Epic: the Mysteries of Her Poetics*, Ann Arbor: UMI Research Press, 1990, 25).
13. Pondrom, 'H.D. and the Origins of Imagism', 95.
14. For an excellent reading of the 'dilemma of subjectivity' in this poem see Buck, *H.D. and Freud*, 29–32.
15. Aldington had enlisted in the army in 1916 and began an affair soon after; during 1915 H.D. became pregnant, but the baby was stillborn.
16. For an analysis of the use of classical myth in this poem see Eileen

Gregory, 'Rose Cut in Rock: Sappho and H.D.'s *Sea Garden*', in Stanford Friedman and DuPlessis (eds.), *Signets*, 148–9.
17. See, for example, Diana Collecott, *H.D. and Sapphic Modernism* (Cambridge: Cambridge University Press, 1999) and the essays by Jaime Hovey and Lilian Fadermann in *Amy Lowell, American Modern*, ed. Adrienne Munich and Melissa Bradshaw (New Brunswick: Rutgers University Press, 2004).
18. Mary E. Galvin, *Queer Poetics: Five Modernist Women Writers* (Westport, CT: Greenwood Press, 1999), 29.
19. Pound certainly saw Lowell's poem, as he arranged for it to be published in *The Egoist*; see Pound, *Selected Letters*, 29.
20. See Preface to Amy Lowell, *Men, Women and Ghosts* (Boston: Houghton Mifflin, 1916), xi.

AFTERWORD

1. Cary Nelson, 'Modern American Poetry', in *The Cambridge Companion to American Modernism*, ed. Walter Kalaidjian (Cambridge University Press, 2005), 72.
2. Pound, *Selected Letters 1907–1941*, ed. D. D. Paige (London: Faber, 1950), 213.
3. Ezra Pound, *The Cantos* (London: Faber, 1981), 428.
4. Pound, 'A Few Don'ts By An Imagiste', *Imagist Poetry*, 130.
5. The title of a popular anthology edited by Harriet Monroe and Alice Corbin Henderson in 1918.
6. For a brief discussion of this poem see Andrew Thacker, 'Unrelated Beauty: Amy Lowell, Polyphonic Prose, and the Imagist City', in *Amy Lowell, American Modern*, ed. Adrienne Munich and Melissa Bradshaw (New Brunswick: Rutgers University Press, 2004).
7. For a discussion of the contradictory ideologies of gender, sexuality and Orientalism in these volumes see Mari Yoshihara, 'Putting on the Voice of the Orient', in Bradshaw and Munich (eds.), *Amy Lowell, American Modern*.
8. *Selected Poems of Amy Lowell*, ed. Melissa Bradshaw and Adrienne Munich (New Brunswick: Rutgers University Press, 2002).
9. The publication of H.D.'s *Collected Poems 1912–1944* (New York: New Directions, 1983), edited by Louis L. Martz, prompted the start of a renewed critical interest in the poet.
10. H.D., 'The Walls Do Not Fall', section 26, *Trilogy* (Cheshire: Carcanet, 1973), 36.
11. Cited in Richard Gray, *American Poetry of the Twentieth Century*, 109. Fletcher, 'Two Elements in Poetry', *Saturday Review of Literature*, 4 (27 August 1927), 65–6. For a consideration of Fletcher's work in a

Southern context see Lucas Carpenter, *John Gould Fletcher and Southern Modernism* (Fayetteville: University of Arkansas Press, 1990).
12. Gray, *American Poetry*, 66.
13. See Louis Zukofsky, 'An Objective', repr. in his *Prepositions: The Collected Critical Essays* (Berkeley: University of California Press, 1981), 14–15. One difference between Zukofsky's work and Imagism is his stress upon an *aural* rather than visual poetics. For a discussion of the further differences see Tim Woods, *The Poetics of the Limit: Ethics and Politics in Modern and Contemporary American Poetry* (Basingstoke: Palgrave Macmillan, 2002), ch. 1.
14. William Carlos Williams, *Autobiography* (1951), cited in Gray, *Modern American Poetry*, 61.
15. Pound, *Selected Letters*, 49.
16. Oppen, cited in Gray, *Modern American Poetry*, 64.
17. Charles Olson, 'Projective Verse' (1950), in *Selected Writings*, ed. Robert Creely (New York: New Directions, 1966), 16; William Carlos Williams, *Paterson*, (Harmondsworth: Penguin, 1983), Author's Note.
18. Pound, *Selected Letters*, 4, 158.
19. Gray, *Modern American Poetry*, 55.
20. Pound, *Cantos*, LXXXII, p. 525.

Select Bibliography

IMAGIST ANTHOLOGIES

Des Imagistes: An Anthology (London: Poetry Bookshop, 1914).
Some Imagist Poets 1915: An Anthology (Boston and New York: Houghton Mifflin, 1915).
Some Imagist Poets 1916: An Annual Anthology (Boston and New York: Houghton Mifflin, 1916).
Some Imagist Poets 1917: An Annual Anthology (Boston and New York: Houghton Mifflin, 1917).
Imagist Anthology 1930 (London: Chatto and Windus, 1930).
The Imagist Poem: Modern Poetry in Miniature, ed. William Pratt (New York: E. P. Dutton, 1963).
Imagist Poetry, ed. Peter Jones (Harmondsworth: Penguin, 1972).
Imagist Poetry: An Anthology, ed. Bob Blaisdell (New York: Dover Publications, 1999).

OTHER PRIMARY WORKS BY THE IMAGISTS

Aldington, Richard, *The Complete Poems of Richard Aldington* (London: Allen Wingate, 1948).
———— *Medallions* (London: Chatto and Windus, 1930).
———— 'Modern Poetry and the Imagists', *Egoist*, 1 June 1914, 202.
———— 'The Poetry of F. S. Flint', *Egoist*, 1 May 1915, 81.
Doolittle, Hilda (H.D.), *Bid Me to Live* (London: Virago, 1984).
———— *Collected Poems 1912–1944*, ed. Louis L. Martz (New York: New Directions, 1983).
Fletcher, John Gould, *The Dominant City (1911–12)* (London: Max Goshen, 1913).
———— *Irradiations: Sand and Spray* (Boston: Houghton Mifflin, 1915).
———— *Selected Letters*, ed. Leighton Rudolph, Lucas Carpenter and Ethel C. Simpson (Fayetteville: University of Arkansas Press, 1996).
———— 'Miss Lowell's Discovery: Polyphonic Prose', *Poetry*, 6 (April

1915), 35.
Flint, F. S., *In the Net of the Stars* (London: Elkin Matthews, 1909).
────── *Otherworld: Cadences* (London: Poetry Bookshop, 1920).
Hulme, T. E., *Further Speculations*, ed. Samuel Hynes (Minneapolis: University of Minnesota Press, 1955).
────── *Selected Writings*, ed. Patrick McGuinness (Manchester: Carcanet Press, 1998).
────── *Speculations: Essays on Humanism and the Philosophy of Art*, ed. Herbert Read (London: Routledge and Kegan Paul, 1924).
Lowell, Amy, *Can Grande's Castle* (Boston: Houghton Mifflin, 1918).
────── *The Complete Poetical Works of Amy Lowell* (Boston: Houghton Mifflin, 1955).
────── *Men, Women and Ghosts* (Boston and New York: Houghton Mifflin, 1916).
────── *Selected Poems of Amy Lowell*, ed. Melissa Bradshaw and Adrienne Munich (New Brunswick: Rutgers University Press, 2002).
────── *Sword Blades and Poppy Seeds* (London: Macmillan, 1914).
────── *Tendencies in Modern American Poetry* (Boston: Houghton Mifflin, 1917).
Pound, Ezra, *Collected Shorter Poems* (London: Faber, 1984).
────── *Gaudier-Brzeska: A Memoir* (1916; repr. New York: New Directions, 1970).
────── *Literary Essays*, ed. T. S. Eliot (London: Faber, 1954).
────── *Selected Prose 1909–1965*, ed. William Cookson (London: Faber, 1973).

AUTOBIOGRAPHY, BIOGRAPHY AND LETTERS

Aldington, Richard, *Life for Life's Sake* (London: Cassell and Co, 1969).
Ayscough, Florence, *Florence Ayscough and Amy Lowell: Correspondence of a Friendship*, ed. Harley Farnsworth MacNair (Chicago, University of Chicago Press, 1945).
Carr, Helen, *The Verse Revolutionaries: Ezra Pound, H. D. and the Imagists* (London: Jonathan Cape, 2009).
Damon, S. Foster, *Amy Lowell: A Chronicle* (Boston and New York: Houghton Mifflin, 1935).
Doolittle, Hilda (H.D.) *End to Torment: A Memoir of Ezra Pound by H.D.*, ed. Norman Holmes Pearson and Michael King (Manchester: Carcanet, 1980).
────── 'Selected Letters from H.D. to F. S. Flint: A Commentary on the Imagist Period', ed. Cyrena Pondrom, *Contemporary Literature*, 10:4 (1969), 557–69.
Doyle, Charles, *Richard Aldington: A Biography* (London: Macmillan,

1989).
Ferguson, Robert, *The Short Sharp Life of T. E. Hulme* (London: Allen Lane, 2002).
Fletcher, John Gould, *Life Is My Song* (New York/Toronto: Farrar and Rinehart, 1937).
Gould, Jean, *Amy: The World of Amy Lowell and the Imagist Movement* (New York: Dodd, Mead and Co., 1975).
Guest, Barbara, *Herself Defined: The Poet H.D. and her World* (London: Collins, 1985).
Jones, Alan, *The Life and Opinions of T .E. Hulme* (London: Gollancz, 1960).
Lawrence, D. H., *The Letters of D. H. Lawrence and Amy Lowell 1914–1925*, ed. E. Claire Healey and Keith Cushman (Santa Barbara: Black Sparrow Press, 1985).
Pound, Ezra, *Selected Letters 1907–1941*, ed. D. D. Paige (London: Faber, 1950).
────── *Pound/Joyce: The Letters of Ezra Pound to James Joyce, with Pound's Essays on Joyce*, ed. Forrest Read (New York: New Directions, 1967).
────── *The Letters of Ezra Pound to Margaret Anderson: The Little Review Correspondence*, ed. Thomas L. Scott and Melvin J. Frieman (New York: New Directions, 1988).
────── *Ezra Pound and Dorothy Shakespear: Their Letters: 1909–1914* , ed. O. Pound and A. Walton Litz, (London: Faber, 1985).
Stock, Noel, *The Life of Ezra Pound* (Harmondsworth: Penguin Books, 1974).

CRITICISM ON IMAGISM AND SPECIFIC IMAGISTS

Bradshaw, Melissa, 'Outselling the Modernisms of Men: Amy Lowell and the Art of Self-Commodification', *Victorian Poetry*, 38:1 (2000), 141–69.
Breunig, Le Roy C., 'F. S. Flint, Imagism's "Maitre D'Ecole"', *Comparative Literature*, 4:2 (Spring 1952), 118–36.
Brooker, Peter, *A Student's Guide to the Selected Poems of Ezra Pound* (London: Faber, 1979).
Bryher, *Amy Lowell: A Critical Appreciation* (London: Eyre and Spottiswoode, 2nd edn, 1918).
Buck, Clare, *H.D. and Freud: Bisexuality and a Feminine Discourse* (Hemel Hempstead: Harvester Wheatsheaf, 1991).
Burnett, Gary, *H.D. Between Image and Epic: The Mysteries of Her Poetics* (Ann Arbor: UMI Research Press, 1990).
Carpenter, Lucas, *John Gould Fletcher and Southern Modernism* (Lafayette/London: University of Arkansas Press, 1990).

Carr, Helen, 'Imagism and Empire', in H. Booth and N. Rigby (eds.), *Modernism and Empire* (Manchester: Manchester University Press, 2000).
Chasca, Edmund De, *John Gould Fletcher and Imagism* (Columbia: University of Missouri Press, 1978).
Coffman, Stanley K., *Imagism: A Chapter for the History of Modern Poetry* (Oklahoma: Norman Press, 1951).
Collecott, Diana, *H.D. and Sapphic Modernism* (Cambridge: Cambridge University Press, 1999).
Comentale, Edward P., and Andrzej Gasiorek (eds.), *T. E. Hulme and the Question of Modernism* (Aldershot: Ashgate, 2006).
Gage, John T., *In the Arresting Eye: The Rhetoric of Imagism* (Baton Rouge: Louisiana State University Press, 1981).
Gregory, Eileen, *H.D. and Hellenism: Classic Lines* (Cambridge: Cambridge University Press, 1997).
Hallberg, Robert von, 'Libertarian Imagism', *Modernism/Modernity*, 2 (April 1995), 63–79.
Harmer, J. B., *Victory in Limbo: Imagism 1908–1917* (London: Secker and Warburg, 1975).
Hough, Graham, *Image and Experience* (London: Duckworth, 1960).
Hughes, Glenn, *Imagism and the Imagists: A Study in Modern Poetry* (California: Stanford University Press, 1931).
Martin, Wallace, 'The Sources of the Imagist Aesthetic', *PMLA*, 85:2 (1970), 196–204.
Materer, Timothy, 'Ezra Pound Advertises Modernism', in Kevin J. H. Dettmar and Stephen Watt (eds.), *Marketing Modernisms: Self-Promotion, Canonization, Rereading* (Ann Arbor: University of Michigan Press, 1996).
Monro, Harold, 'The Imagists Discussed', *Egoist*, 1 May 1915, 79.
Munich, Adrienne, and Melissa Bradshaw (eds.), *Amy Lowell: American Modern* (New Brunswick: Rutgers University Press, 2004).
Pondrom, Cyrena, 'H.D. and the Origins of Imagism', in Susan Stanford Friedman and Rachel Blau DuPlessis (eds.), *Signets: Reading H.D.* (Madison: University of Wisconsin Press, 1990), 86.
Pratt, William, and Robert Richardson (eds.), *Homage to Imagism* (New York: AMS Press, 1992).
Randall, Bryony, 'John Gould Fletcher's City Aesthetic: "London Excursion"', *Literary London*, 4:1 (2006), 7, www.literarylondon.org/london-journal/randall.html.
Ruthven, K. K., *A Guide to Ezra Pound's 'Personae' (1926)* (Berkeley: University of California Press, 1969).
Sedgwick III, Ellery, '"Fireworks": Amy Lowell and the Atlantic Monthly', *New England Quarterly*, 51:4 (December 1978), 489–508.
Stead, C. K., *The New Poetic: Yeats to Eliot* (Harmondsworth: Penguin,

1967).

Thacker, Andrew, 'Imagist Travels', in *Moving Through Modernity: Space, Geography and Modernism* (Manchester: Manchester University Press, 2003).

────── ' "Mad After Foreign Notions": Ezra Pound, Imagism and the Geography of the Orient', in Peter Brooker and Andrew Thacker (eds.), *Geographies of Modernism: Literatures, Cultures, Spaces* (Abingdon: Routledge, 2005).

Wilhelm, J. J., *Ezra Pound in London and Paris 1908–1925* (Philadelphia: Penn State University Press, 1990).

BACKGROUND

Apollonia, Umbro (ed.), *Futurist Manifestos* (London: Thames and Hudson, 1973).

Bergson, Henri, *An Introduction to Metaphysics*, (1903; trans. T. E. Hulme, London: Macmillan, 1913).

Binyon, Laurence, *Painting in the Far East: An Introduction to the History of Pictorial Art in Asia: Especially China and India* (London: Edward Arnold, 1908).

Bradbury, Malcolm, and James McFarlane (eds.), *Modernism: A Guide to European Literature 1890–1930* (Harmondsworth: Penguin, 1976).

Brooker, Peter, *Bohemia in London: The Social Scene of Early Modernism* (Basingstoke: Palgrave, 2004).

Brooker, Peter, and Andrew Thacker (eds.), *The Oxford Critical and Cultural History of Modernist Magazines. Volume I, Britain and Ireland 1880–1955* (Oxford: Oxford University Press, 2009).

Clarke, Bruce, *Dora Marsden and Early Modernism: Gender, Individualism, Science* (Ann Arbor: University of Michigan Press, 1996).

Comentale, Edward P., *Modernism, Cultural Production, and the British Avant-Garde* (Cambridge: Cambridge University Press, 2004).

Emig, Rainer, *Modernism in Poetry: Motivations, Structures and Limits* (London: Longman, 1995).

Fenollosa, Ernest, *The Chinese Written Character as a Medium for Poetry*, ed. Ezra Pound (San Francisco: City Lights, 1969).

Galvin, Mary E., *Queer Poetics: Five Modernist Women Writers* (Westport, CT: Greenwood Press, 1999).

Garner, Les, *A Brave and Beautiful Spirit: Dora Marsden, 1882–1960* (Avebury: Gower Publishing, 1990).

Georgian Poetry, 1911–12 (London: Poetry Bookshop, 1912).

Grant, Joy, *Harold Monro and the Poetry Bookshop* (London: Routledge and Kegan Paul, 1967).

Hanscombe, Gillian, and Virginia L. Smyers, *Writing for their Lives: The*

Modernist Woman 1910–1940 (London: Women's Press, 1987).
Hoffman, Frederick J., Charles Allen, and Carolyn F. Ulrich, *The Little Magazine: A History and a Bibliography* (New Jersey: Princeton University Press, 1947).
Kenner, Hugh, *The Pound Era*, (Berkeley/Los Angeles: University of California Press, 1971).
Kodama, S. (ed.), *Ezra Pound and Japan: Letters and Essays* (Redding Ridge, CT: Black Swan Books, 1987).
Levenson, Michael H., *A Genealogy of Modernism: A Study of English Literary Doctrine 1908–1922* (Cambridge: Cambridge University Press, 1984).
Lyon, Janet, *Manifestos: Provocations of the Modern* (Ithaca and London: Cornell University Press, 1999).
McDonald, Peter, 'Modernist Publishing', in David Bradshaw (ed.), *A Concise Companion to Modernism* (Oxford: Blackwell, 2003).
Michel, Walter, and C. J. Fox (eds.), *Wyndham Lewis on Art: Collected Writings, 1913–1956* (New York: Funk and Wagnalls, 1969).
Morrison, Mark,*The Public Face of Modernism: Little Magazines, Audiences, and Reception, 1905–1920* (Madison: University of Wisconsin Press, 2001).
Nelson, James G., *Elkin Mathews: Publisher to Yeats, Joyce, Pound* (Madison: Wisconsin University Press, 1989).
Nicholls, Peter, *Modernisms: A Literary Guide* (Basingstoke: Macmillan, 1995).
Noguchi, Yone, *Selected Writings of Yone Noguchi: An East-West Literary Assimilation*, vol. 2, *Prose*, ed. Y. Hakutani (London and Toronto: Fairleigh Dickinson University Press, 1992).
——— 'What is a Hokku Poem?' *Rhythm*, 12 (January 1913), 354–9.
Parker, Rennie, *The Georgian Poets* (Plymouth: Northcote House, 1998).
Parsons, Deborah L., *Streetwalking the City: Women, the City and Modernity* (Oxford: Oxford University Press, 2000).
Pondrom, Cyrena N., *The Road from Paris: French Influence on English Poetry, 1900–1920* (Cambridge: Cambridge University Press, 1974).
Pound, Ezra, 'Small Magazines', *English Journal*, 19:9 (November 1930), 689–704.
Qian, Zhaoming, *Orientalism and Modernism: The Legacy of China in Pound and Williams* (Durham: Duke University Press,1995).
Rainey, Lawrence, *Institutions of Modernism: Literary Elites and Public Culture* (New Haven/London: Yale University Press, 1998).
Schwartz, Sanford, *The Matrix of Modernism: Pound, Eliot, and Early Twentieth-Century Thought* (Princeton, NJ: Princeton University Press, 1985).
Stansky, Peter, *On or About December 1910: Early Bloomsbury and Its Intimate World* (Cambridge, MA: Harvard University Press, 1997).
Tate, Trudi, *Modernism, History and the First World War* (Manchester:

Manchester University Press, 1998).
Thacker, Andrew, '"Our War Is With Words": Dora Marsden and *The Egoist*', in Gabriele Griffin (ed.), *Difference in View: Women and Modernism* (London: Taylor and Francis, 1994).

Index

'A Few Don'ts by an Imagiste'
  37, 40, 44–7, 50, 69, 103
Aldington, Richard 1, 4, 5, 8–9,
  10, 11, 16–18, 20, 22, 25, 29,
  30, 32, 34, 35, 36, 48, 55, 62,
  68, 70, 72, 74, 75, 83, 89, 91,
  92–3, 94, 95, 96, 105
  'Eros and Psyche' 72
  'In the Tube' 68
  'Sunsets' 8–9
  'Whitechapel' 72
Anderson, Margaret 33
Anyte of Tegea 92
Ayscough, Florence 65, 104

Bakhtin, Mikhail 52
Baudelaire, Charles 103
Bergson, Henri 10, 42–3, 55
Binyon, Laurence 59–60, 62, 63
Blaisdell, Bob 24
Blast 15
Brooke, Rupert 17
Bryher 84–5, 89, 94
Bunting, Basil 105
Bynner, Witter 20

Campbell, Joseph 11
Cannell, Skipworth 4, 5
Carr, Helen 59–60, 66
Carter, Huntley 29
China and Chinese culture 58–66
Conrad, Joseph 12
Cournos, John 4, 64

Cubism 2, 12, 30, 78
cultural formations 3, 7, 11, 15,
  18–19, 22, 37, 38, 41, 49, 88,
  89, 101, 108

Dada 12, 19, 26
De Gourmont, Remy 29
Des Imagistes 3, 5, 6, 11, 15–16, 17,
  20, 21, 22, 24, 25, 30, 47, 64,
  70
Dolmetsch, Arnold 50
Doolittle, Hilda (H. D.) 1, 2, 4, 5,
  10, 11, 17, 20, 25, 30, 34, 35,
  36, 45, 47, 57–8, 62, 66, 70–1,
  74, 88, 89–101, 104–5,
  Bid Me to Live 74
  'Cities' 88
  Collected Poems (1983) 2
  'The Garden' 94–5
  'Hermes of the Ways' 30, 62,
    71, 92–3
  'Mid-day' 95–6
  'Oread' 57–8
  'The Pool' 45, 47, 93–4, 100
  'Pygmalion' 96
  'Temple – The Cliff' 95
  Trilogy 104–5

The Egoist 3, 15, 20, 24, 25, 26, 27–
  36, 37, 42, 46, 62, 68, 70, 77,
  99
Eliot, T. S. 1, 22, 35, 58, 75, 78, 82
Ellmann, Richard 24

Farr, Florence 11, 50–1
Fenollosa, Ernest 59, 63, 64, 66
Fenollosa, Mary 64
Fitzgerald, Desmond 11
Fletcher, John Gould 1, 2, 4, 5, 17, 20, 25, 30, 31–3, 34, 35, 39, 40, 47, 48, 49, 50, 51–2, 56, 57, 65–6, 67, 68, 75–80, 83, 84, 87, 88, 90, 105, 106
Goblins and Pagodas 66
Japanese Prints 66
'London Excursion' 68, 77–80, 84, 87
'The Skaters' 56–7
'The Empty House' 76–7
'The Unquiet Street' 76
Flint, F. S. 1, 2, 4, 10, 11, 12, 17, 18, 20, 25, 30, 33, 34, 35, 40–2, 47, 61, 66, 67, 68, 70–5, 78, 106
'Accident' 68
'Hallucination' 30
'London' 70–1
'Searchlight' 73–4
'Tube' 68
'War-Time' 72–3
'Zeppelins' 74–5
Ford, Ford Madox 1, 2, 4, 5, 12, 14, 31, 33, 42, 48, 108
Fort, Paul 51
The Freewoman (see *The Egoist*)
Freud, Sigmund 58, 77, 91
Fugitives 105
Futurism 2, 3, 11, 12, 15, 17–20, 23, 28, 37–8, 39, 40, 41, 49, 52, 53, 82

Gage, John T. 56, 57
Galvin, Mary 99
Gawthorpe, Mary 27
gender 89–101
Georgian poets 11, 16–17, 22, 37–8, 41
Giles, H. A. 60, 61

Gissing, George 13, 32
New Grub Street 13–14, 32
The Glebe 3, 24, 30
Goldring, Douglas 11
Gray, Richard 105, 107
Greenslet, Ferris 34, 35
Gregg, Frances 89, 94

Harmer, J. B. 25
Hoffman, F. 26
Housman, A. E. 17
Hughes, Glenn 39
Hulme, T. E. 10–11, 12, 17, 28, 37, 42–7, 48, 50, 53, 54–6, 57, 61, 66, 69, 90–1, 93, 95, 107, 108
'Above the Dock' 44–5, 47
'Romanticism and Classicism' 54–5, 91

'Imagisme' 37, 39, 40–2, 44, 47, 49, 54, 102
Imagist Anthology 1930 5
Imagist Poetry 1, 12
Impressionism 2, 11–12

Jameson, Fredric 86
Japan and Japanese culture 58–66
Jones, Peter 1, 12, 24
Joyce, James 1, 4, 6, 12, 15, 24, 26, 28, 30, 33, 35, 80–1, 85
'I Hear an Army' 4, 6, 15

Kenner, Hugh 27, 67

Lawrence, D. H. 1, 4, 12, 17, 20, 33, 34
Le Gallienne, Richard 7–9,
Lewis, Percy Wyndham 2, 12, 20, 30, 35, 38
little magazines 24–36
The Little Review 14, 25, 33, 35
Lowell, Amy 1, 2, 4, 5–6, 15, 17, 18, 19–23, 24, 25, 30, 31, 32–5,

132

36, 37, 47–52, 65–6, 67, 80–8, 89–91, 96–101, 102, 104, 106, 108
'A Decade' 98
'Astigmatism' 97
'Aubade' 99–100
'The Basket' 96–7
Can Grande's Castle 104
'In Excelsis' 97–8
Fir-Flower Tablets 65, 104
'Frimaire' 98
'Guns as Keys' 65
'Lacquer Prints' 65
Men, Women and Ghosts 52, 84
Pictures of the Floating World 65, 98, 104
'Planes of Personality: Two Speak Together' 98
'Spring Day' 52, 80–5
'Sultry' 96
Sword Blades and Poppy Seeds 97
'Towns in Colour' 85–7
'The Weather-Cock Points South' 98–9, 100
Lyon, Janet 38–40

Marek, Jayne 23, 34
Marinetti, F. T. 3, 11, 17–19, 39, 63, 64
Marsden, Dora 27–9, 32, 36
Marsh, Edward 16, 17, 37
Mathews, Elkin 62
McDonald, Peter 24–5
Monro, Harold 16, 17, 19, 25, 35, 77
Monroe, Harriet 6, 21, 25, 29, 48, 53, 92, 105, 106
Morrisson, Mark 14, 15, 26–7, 28

Nelson, Cary 102
The New Age 12, 25, 40, 64
The New Freewoman (see *The Egoist*)

Noguchi, Yone 62

Objectivism 12, 54, 105–8
Olson, Charles 107
Oppen, George 105–7
  'Bad Times' 106–7
orientalism 58–66

Pater, Walter 13, 50
Poetry 3, 6, 10, 25, 29, 32, 37, 45, 105
The Poetry Review 10, 16, 25, 28, 40, 42
The Poetry Bookshop 3, 16, 18, 19
polyphonic prose 2, 47, 50–2, 65, 67, 80–7, 100, 104
Pondrom, Cyrena 90, 92
Post-Impressionism 11, 12, 14, 40, 41, 78
Pound, Ezra 1, 2, 3, 4, 5, 6, 9, 10, 12, 15–16, 17, 18, 19–22, 24, 25–6, 29, 30–6, 39–42, 44, 45–51, 53–66, 67–70, 79, 82, 83, 88, 89–90, 91–2, 94, 95, 96, 97, 99–100, 101, 102–4, 105, 106–7, 108
  'Alba' 99–100
  The Cantos 65, 102–4, 108
  'The Encounter' 58, 61
  'Fan Piece, for her Imperial Lord' 60–1
  'Further Instructions' 58–9
  'In a Station of the Metro' 67–9, 88, 106, 107
  'Liu Ch'e' 30
  A Lume Spento 15
  'The Return' 71
  'Ts'ai Chi'h' 55–6, 57, 103
  'Vorticism' 58
Pratt, William 24

Qian, Zhaoming 60, 61, 64

Rakosi, Carl 105
Rainey, Lawrence 3, 4, 14, 18, 20, 63, 64
Randall, Bryony 78
Reznikoff, Charles 105
Rhymers' Club 10, 46
Rhythm 62
Roberts, William 12
Romains, Jules 12
Russell, Ada 89, 98

Sedgwick, Ellery 34
sexuality 89–101
Shakespeare, Dorothy 64
Simmel, Georg 69, 88
Sinclair, May 37, 46
The Smart Set 99
Some Imagist Poets 1915 4, 6, 21–22, 34, 35, 45, 48–9, 53, 77, 80
Some Imagist Poets 1916 4, 8, 49–50, 72, 76
Some Imagist Poets 1917 4, 96
Stead, C. K. 1
Stirner, Max 28
Storer, Edward 11
Stravinsky, Igor 82

Symbolism 7, 12, 60
Symons, Arthur 12, 46

Tancred, Francis 11
Tennyson, Alfred Lord 13
Thomas, Edward 17

Upward, Allen 4, 29, 60–1, 64

vers libre (free verse) 8, 11, 40, 47, 50, 51, 61, 71–2
Vorticism 2, 12, 15, 20, 23, 26, 38, 39, 52, 58, 82

Weaver, Harriet Shaw 28, 65
West, Rebecca 28
Wilde, Oscar 13
Williams, Raymond 18–19, 43, 83
Williams, William Carlos 1, 4, 71, 105, 106, 107
Wilson, Elizabeth 69, 77
Woolf, Virginia 85

Yeats, W. B. 10, 17, 33, 50, 65

Zukofsky, Louis 105–6, 107

www.ingramcontent.com/pod-product-compliance
Ingram Content Group UK Ltd.
Pitfield, Milton Keynes, MK11 3LW, UK
UKHW041419180426
11947UKWH00007B/207